The Master's Plan for
Making Disciples

THE MASTER'S PLAN FOR MAKING DISCIPLES

by Win Arn
and Charles Arn

Nazarene Version
by Bill M. Sullivan

Nazarene Publishing House
Kansas City, Missouri

© Copyright 1982 by Church Growth Press
709 East Colorado, No. 150, Pasadena, CA 91101

Nazarene Version, 1984
Printed by Nazarene Publishing House

ISBN: 0-8341-0938-7

Printed in the
United States of America

Unless otherwise indicated, all Scripture quotations are from *The Holy Bible, New International Version* (NIV), copyright © 1978 by the New York International Bible Society, and are used by permission.

Permission to quote from other copyrighted versions of the Bible is acknowledged with appreciation:

The Living Bible (TLB), © 1971 by Tyndale House Publishers, Wheaton, Ill.
    Used by permission.
The *New English Bible* (NEB), © The Delegates of the Oxford University
    Press and The Syndics of the Cambridge University Press, 1961, 1970.
    Used by permission.

10 9 8 7 6 5 4 3 2 1

Contents

Preface 7

Introduction 9

1 The Master's Plan—Making Disciples 11

2 How New Disciples Are Made—
the *Oikos* Factor 24

3 Incorporation—the Entry Essential
for Making Disciples 41

4 Key Principles of Disciple-making 51

5 Seven Steps for Making Disciples 61

6 Planning for Conversion in the
Disciple-making Process 74

7 Reaching Your "Extended Family" 84

8 Your Church—Partner in Disciple-making 96

9 Assimilating New Disciples into the Church 108

10 The Master's Plan—to the Ends of the Earth 117

Glossary 129

Reference Notes 133

Preface
About the Nazarene Version

We have planned since 1980 that the CLT denomination-wide study for the Year of Church Growth would focus on web evangelism—reaching relatives, friends, and associates who make up our webs of influence. There was some conversation about a joint development of the plan with Dr. Win Arn, but other priorities prevented our participation.

When Dr. Win Arn and Charles Arn published *The Master's Plan for Making Disciples* in 1982 we recognized that it was the book for the 1985 CLT text. We immediately began negotiating for approval to publish a Nazarene version. They have been very helpful in facilitating our own church version.

Appreciation is expressed not only to Drs. Arn and Arn but also to Dr. David Holtz, who began the abridgment; Mrs. Nina Beegle, who did general editing and some rewriting in Chapters 4 and 7; and especially to Miss Nancy Lytle, who typed the manuscript many times and coordinated the project. Several others in the Division of Church Growth have made helpful suggestions.

We believe this edition is a worthwhile contribution to the literature on evangelism in the local church. We think Nazarenes will find *The Master's Plan* to be the plan that fits them best.

Introduction

Evangelism is making disciples. Some organizations are willing to settle for less. Not the Church of the Nazarene. We are not satisfied with just telling people about Jesus Christ. We want them to repent and believe the gospel. Even this is not enough. We want more than decisions. Our goal is nothing less than growing Christians who are actively involved in the fellowship, ministry, and task of a local church.

We pursue revival—but not for its own sake. The renewal of spiritual fervor is to provide energy for evangelism, and our revivals are seasons of harvest when new people are converted and young Christians are sanctified wholly. Every year thousands of revivals fulfill a critical phase of the denomination's commitment to a broad concept of evangelism.

Outreach and friendship, which precede conversion, are other phases of the disciple-making process. Education, training, and involvement are phases of the process that follow conversion. All phases are important and require intentional activity. This is the evangelism the Church of the Nazarene believes in and the only approach with which we are truly at home.

We use many methods to help us with the total process. But we know instinctively that the task is not complete until we have growing, serving Christians. On occasion we become enthusiastic about novel programs and contemporary techniques, but we maintain them only if they truly contribute to the ultimate goal.

We are making disciples. We know the importance of transformation, for we are new creatures in Christ Jesus. Apart from God's saving grace, we are nothing. Our commitment to Christian education is strong, and we recognize that it is a task that is never complete. Since our educational objectives are life application, training is a high priority. We stress involvement in Christian witness and ministry to the needs of others. We give strong emphasis to missions. The goal is very clear—make disciples all over the world.

The Great Commission compels us. Three billion unreached people challenge every resource we can lay hold of. World evangelization is at the heart of our denominational unity. We join hearts and hands in hope that somehow we can be equal to our part of the total assignment.

To accomplish our mission, total participation is essential. Everyone must be involved—praying, working, and witnessing. How fortunate we are to have found a plan that involves everyone in a very natural, yet intentional process of witnessing. Not forced confrontation of strangers but natural involvement with friends. A plan as old as the church, yet as up-to-date as the latest opinion poll. It's a plan that works every day, week after week and year after year. It is *The Master's Plan for Making Disciples*. It fits us—who we are, what we believe about evangelism, and the way we prefer to accomplish it.

It is natural but it includes intentionality. There is just the right amount of structure, enough to sustain it and increase our evangelistic effectiveness.

It is comprehensive, spanning from the first contact through the crises and processes to involvement in the mission of the church. It is disciple-making in the fullest sense of the term.

The Master's Plan will be welcomed by Nazarenes. Our people are eager to find ways of more effectively sharing their faith and participating in the task of the Great Commission. *The Master's Plan* is just what we have been looking for, and this plan will enable us to more effectively share the message that a lost world is waiting for.

BILL M. SULLIVAN
Church Growth Division Director

1

The Master's Plan—
Making Disciples

Wearily Chuck Bradley turned to his wife. "Diane, I'm not going . . . and that's final!"

"But, Chuck, I promised you'd go with me," replied Diane.

"Don't I have the right to make up my own mind?"

"Well, sure you do, sweetheart, but I just assumed you'd be interested in learning more about evangelism."

"Please, Diane, don't try to make me feel guilty!"

"But just think how it will look if I go alone. People will say, 'Chuck Bradley doesn't care about sharing his faith.'"

Chuck did not like the direction this conversation was taking. "Diane, you know that's not true. I do care about evangelism, as much as anybody. I just don't care about another 'witnessing seminar.'"

"But, Chuck, Pastor Austin said this would be different."

"Well, of course he'd say that. Diane, I'm just tired of trying to learn one new method after another for witnessing. You'd think we were some kind of door-to-door salespeople."

"But, Chuck, you do believe that Christians ought to share their faith?"

"You know I do . . . but I'm just not sure Jesus is supposed to be marketed by people acting like Fuller Brush men and Avon ladies. Besides, I haven't had much success with

"Remember the summer we went camping ... and I tried out my new witnessing training," Chuck retorted.

those kinds of methods anyway. Remember the summer we went camping . . . and I tried out my new witnessing training?"

"Yes, Chuck, I know. But, a few bad experiences don't give you the right to stop witnessing."

"You're absolutely right, Diane. But at this moment I have a very hard time believing that anything I say . . . as a witness . . . will really make a difference in another person's life."

"But if you went with me tonight maybe you'd learn something that would help," pleaded Diane.

"No, Diane. When it comes to witnessing, I feel just like one of those disciples who fished all night and caught absolutely nothing!"

* * * * * * * * *

How do you feel about sharing your faith? There are a lot of Christians who feel as Chuck did. Although they believe in evangelism, their personal efforts have had little or no results. Like the disciples, they have "fished all night and caught nothing."

But remember that's not the end of the story. Let's refresh our memories.

The first rays of a new morning sun peeked over the eastern sunburned hills. Stretching out for miles below lies a quiet, mirrorlike blue lake. A few hundred yards offshore a solitary boat appears fastened to the still surface. Periodically one of the two figures in the 20-foot wooden boat stands and stretches. The motionless air carries the occasional morning wake-up call of a rooster across the water.

Finally, the men begin to pull in their nets, causing ripples of disturbed water to ring their way toward shore. The splash from wet nets breaks the morning silence. The fishermen eagerly search their nets for the product of their nocturnal labors. But as the last empty net is piled onto the boat bottom, they discouragingly reach for the oars. Another wasted night.

"How's the fishing?" a man calls from the shore.

After a pause, a frustrated voice replies, "Nothing. Absolutely nothing!"

"Throw your nets on the other side of the boat," orders the man on shore.

"But we've fished all night." Then, after a long pause, and sensing an authority in the voice, a fisherman responds, "All right, but only once more."

Shortly they retrieve their nets from the same water, and shouts of excitement ring out. Calls for help sound from the boat—help to bring in the nets that are so full they are beginning to break!

What a moment that must have been! Peter and Andrew trying desperately to bring in the catch, excitedly shouting to their fellow fishermen. Yet, what mind-stretching questions must have raced through their heads! How had Jesus, from offshore, known where the fish were? Was it a miracle? It must have been! But how? Why?

As they pulled the wiggly, flopping fish into the boat, Jesus' words of long ago to Peter suddenly echoed in his mind: "Come, follow me, . . . and I will make you fishers of men" (Matt. 4:19).

During His life on earth, our Master gave us a plan for successful fishing, a model for making disciples. There is a vast potential catch available on "the other side of the boat," if we follow His plan. It is a way that can result in many new people coming into a life-changing relationship with Christ and His Church. A plan that results in a new spiritual dimension in our own lives, new effectiveness in making disciples, new ministry and growth for our churches in fulfilling His command to "Go and make disciples."

The Master's Plan—God's Purpose

"For God so loved the world that he gave his one and only Son, that whoever believes in him shall not perish but have eternal life. For God did not send his Son into the world to condemn the world, but to save the world through him" (John 3:16-17).

But how could the world that God so loved ever hear and believe such an awesome act of love? Jesus, in a conversation with His Father, supplies the answer: "As you sent me into the world, I have sent them into the world . . . that the world may believe that you have sent me (John 17:18, 21). The Lord made His disciples' task crystal clear: "You will be my witnesses in Jerusalem, and in all Judea and Samaria, and to the ends of the earth" (Acts 1:8).

What were they to "witness" about? Again, Christ was specific and direct: "This is what is written: The Christ will suffer and rise from the dead on the third day, and repentance

14

and forgiveness of sins will be preached in his name to all nations, beginning at Jerusalem. You are witnesses of these things" (Luke 24:46-48).

God, speaking to us through Scripture, presents a startlingly clear statement of His desire and unswerving purpose that lost mankind be reached and brought into His fellowship. Christ's birth, crucifixion, and resurrection were for the purpose of reconciling men and women with their Creator. Passage after passage in the Bible clearly underscores God's will "who wants all men to be saved and to come to a knowledge of the truth" (1 Tim. 2:4).

The Master's Plan—the Commission

In a final summary of His earthly life and purpose, Christ turned over His own commission from God to His followers. As His Father had sent Him, so He was sending them (see John 20:21). It was a life-encompassing challenge that could not be misinterpreted: "Therefore go and make disciples of all nations, baptizing them in the name of the Father and of the Son and of the Holy Spirit, and teaching them to obey everything I have commanded you" (Matt. 28:19-20).

This great commission to His followers, repeated on several occasions, reflects God's eternal purpose that all people everywhere have the opportunity to become disciples of Jesus Christ. It was this command of God through Jesus Christ that exerted singular direction on the Early Church. Central in all of Christ's teaching was the assumption that to follow Him meant to become participants in His mission.[1] When Christ gave the church its final directive, there was no question but that this command was to be given top priority.

The expectation that all who received Jesus Christ as Lord and Savior would become His faithful and active disciples appears to have been widely held by first-century Christians. What the apostle Paul affirmed, they virtually assumed was true of themselves: "We are therefore Christ's ambassadors, as though God were making his appeal through us. We implore you on Christ's behalf: Be reconciled to God" (2 Cor. 5:20).

Being His follower assumed not only an active commitment to His Lordship, but also included active involvement in the propagation of His gospel. By definition, disciples became "fishers of men." Christ's central desire for His disciples was that, when He was gone, they would have ingrained in their hearts and minds the conviction that the Son of Man had come to seek and to save those who were lost. His words, recorded in Matt. 28:19-20, now called the Great Commission, were simply a restatement of His entire life and teaching. He made the directive as simple and easy to understand as possible, "Go and make disciples" (Matt. 28:19).

The Master's Plan—Make Disciples

His Great Commission communicates vividly Christ's understanding of a disciple. He saw a disciple as one who becomes a follower, who is taught, who is nurtured in the faith, who in turn goes out to make disciples, who are then taught and nurtured in the faith, who in turn go out . . .

The perpetual multiplying of disciples reflects Christ's strategy for reaching "the ends of the earth." This strategy, as Luke records, became the basis of the explosive growth of the Early Church: "the number of disciples was increasing" (Acts 6:1); and "the number of disciples in Jerusalem increased rapidly" (v. 7); the churches "encouraged by the Holy Spirit . . . grew in numbers" (9:31).

Christ expects every disciple to share his faith. Acts 1:8 says, "You will be my witnesses." The Greek verb in this command is actually in the declarative form. Had Christ used the imperative verb "to be," it would have implied a conscious activity or planned action. Rather, Christ meant that *being* His witness was a natural, assumed part of the disciple's lifestyle. This is God's secret to fulfilling the Great Commission!

The Master's Plan—as Followed by the Early Church

The gospel was shared so that people all around the world would have faith in Christ and obey Him (see Rom. 16:26). And Luke records that people did respond in faith and obedience: "So the word of God spread. The number of disciples in Jerusalem increased rapidly, and a large number of priests became obedient to the faith" (Acts 6:7).

What underlying principles caused those first-century Christians to achieve such remarkable success in making disciples?

1. *The Goal Was Clear—Make Disciples.* Being a disciple in the Early Church meant a firsthand involvement in the mission of Christ—making disciples. The goal was clear and all-encompassing.

This goal would continually expand the base of new disciples. In the book *Back to Basics* the authors note that "inherent in being saved was that the redeemed share the Good News. Being a Christian meant worshiping God; it meant doing good to all men, especially those of the household of faith. It meant expecting the Lord to return. It meant sins forgiven. *But above and beyond these, it meant telling people that the Savior had come—*that eternal life was theirs by repentance and faith in Him."[2]

A new convert's commitment to Christ included the assumption that he reproduce himself and continue in the disciple-making chain. New disciples were instruments used by the Holy Spirit to make disciples.

2. *Every Christian—a Witness.* Inherent in the definition of a "disciple" was one who shared the Good News with others. First-century Christians told the story of Christ simply and graciously. Each believer's actions and attitudes confirmed the centrality of Christ in his life. Christians vouched for the way the Lord had met all their needs. Naturally and

winsomely, these Christians told of "the hope that was within them," presenting a convincing witness.

Although fellowship with members of the Body was a vital part of their lives, believers did not remain in the "holy huddle." Scripture records that everywhere they journeyed, early Christians witnessed to the claims of Christ. While there are only three references in the New Testament to those who are "evangelists" (with the special gift of evangelism), Scripture contains over 120 references to the broader commission to all members of the Church to preach the gospel and make disciples.[3] The early Christians did not discount the command of making disciples on the claim that they lacked the gift of evangelist. By naturally communicating their faith, they became God's instruments for bringing many people into His kingdom.

3. *Compassion—Permeating the Mission.* The early Christians knew the deep concern their Lord had for "lost sheep." He loved Matthew and Zacchaeus—despised tax collectors; He loved Roman centurions—the hated overlords of Judea; He loved lepers; He loved the blind, the lame, the halt. Christ's love for the multitudes, the children, the outcasts of society must have been told and retold by the first believers.

The Early Church mirrored its Master's compassion. The church was a loving, caring community. Their compassion in the routine of everyday living is seen in the many garments Dorcas made and gave to the poor (see Acts 9:39); the sharing of property and possession, according to need (see Acts 2:45).

In writing to the Corinthians, Paul warned, "If I speak in the tongues of men and of angels, but have not love, I am only a resounding gong or a clanging cymbal" (1 Cor. 13:1). As the normal fruit of the Spirit, compassion was one of the seeds of New Testament church growth.[4]

4. *Relationships—the Means for Sharing the Master's Love.* The process by which the Early Church grew so ex-

plosively was through the individual Christian's interlocking social system—the family, friends, and associates. Christ often commanded new believers to return to their "households" (friends and family) and tell them of the Good News. Michael Green, in *Evangelism and the Early Church,* observes that the New Testament church religiously adhered to the strategy of using *"households"* in the Christian advance.[5] Luke records how those in the homes of Christians responded to the gospel, with the result that "the Lord added to their number daily those who were being saved" (Acts 2:47).

Why were these households of friends and family so receptive to the gospel? Two reasons: First, the caring and love that characterized household relationships implied a level of trust, friendship, and common concern. In the household, a person's concerns and convictions were respected and listened to. Second, those intimate with the new believer could witness the reality of a life changed by the power of the Master's love. Such a change in a person's life-style naturally had a significant impact on one's friends and family.

The early Christians knew that when the message of God's love was heard and demonstrated by those who were known and trusted, the barriers of distrust and suspicion lowered, and receptivity to the Good News increased tremendously. Thus, the Good News of God's love moved quickly and naturally along the lines of relationships.

5. *The Mission—Directed and Empowered by the Holy Spirit.* These Christians knew their source of strength—the Holy Spirit who empowered them to live up to the high calling left by Christ Jesus. The Holy Spirit is revealed as the great strategist throughout Acts. He is indisputably the Superintendent of the great missionary endeavor. He empowers and initiates, guides and directs. Jesus specifically told them to wait for the Holy Spirit because He would give them power to be witnesses in Jerusalem, Judea, Samaria, and the ends of the

world (Acts 1:8). "With great power the apostles continued to testify to the resurrection of the Lord Jesus, and much grace was upon them all" (Acts 4:33).

Evidence of the direct effusion and guidance of the Spirit abounds in the Acts of the Apostles. One recalls how Philip, after having been significantly used by the Spirit to bring many Samaritans to Christ, was guided to reach an Ethiopian eunuch with the gospel (see Acts 8:29).

And the beginnings of the evangelization of the Gentiles was likewise under the Spirit's direction: "While Peter was still thinking about the vision, the Spirit said to him, 'Simon, three men are looking for you. So get up and go downstairs. Do not hesitate to go with them, for I have sent them'" (Acts 10:19-20).

The Holy Spirit continued as an active part of the spread of the gospel: "While they were worshiping the Lord and fasting, the Holy Spirit said, 'Set apart for me Barnabas and Saul for the work to which I have called them'" (Acts 13:2).

The pages of the New Testament tell again and again of men and women who, through faith in Jesus Christ, were given access through the Spirit to the Father. Filled with unshakable certainty that God had, through Christ, opened the way of salvation, they multiplied churches throughout the land.

6. *Boldness—in the Extension of the Faith.* In the forum in Rome, in Ephesus, in Lystra, the Scriptures do not portray Paul possessed with the spirit of compromise or timidity (see Eph. 6:19). Instead, we read of the courageous yet loving proclamations made here and there by an ambassador of the one true God. Paul preached his message fearlessly, even though he was frequently mobbed, beaten, and ridiculed.

Boldness was no more a natural or inherent trait of the early Christians than it is today. The apostles needed to pray often for boldness in preaching (see Acts 4:29).

"After they prayed, the place where they were meeting was shaken. And they were all filled with the Holy Spirit and spoke the word of God boldly" (Acts 4:31). And Scripture testifies to the fruits of this intense desire to communicate the Good News, no matter what the cost. "When they saw the courage of Peter and John and realized that they were unschooled, ordinary men, they were astonished" (Acts 4:13).

7. *The Scriptures—a Reference Point.* Wherever these early believers went, they spread *the Word.* Luke refers to the expansion of the church, by telling us that *the Word grew. The Word* means, of course, their proclamation of Jesus on the basis of the Old Testament.

The apostles, grounded in the Old Testament scriptures, knew their Jewish audience regarded the scriptures as absolute truth. "For it is written" held the potential for convincing even the Jewish skeptics. Again and again these disciple-makers pointed to Christ's birth, life, death, resurrection, and ascension as the fulfillment of Old Testament prophecy; that God's eternal promise to reconcile mankind to himself had at last been fulfilled (see Acts 13:32-35).

In dealing with those of Jewish background, early Christians had a strong preference for particular passages in the Old Testament. Psalm 110 was one of the most favored. They immersed themselves in *the Word,* studying and thinking out how they would proclaim it.

Knowing that God had spoken partially through the Old Testament scripture and now spoke fully and completely through Jesus Christ, they searched the Old Testament scriptures for insights concerning the Messiah.

8. *The Church—a Body of Believers.* The New Testament frequently pictures the disciple of Christ in a group setting; a sheep in a flock, a soldier in the army, a limb in the body, a stone in a building.[6] Becoming a member of the Early Church was a shared corporate experience. "Every day they

continued to meet together in the temple courts. They broke bread in their homes and ate together with glad and sincere hearts, praising God and enjoying the favor of all the people" (Acts 2:46-47).

They recognized that by meeting together the Body derived strength, encouragement, stimulation, and knowledge. "Let us hold unswervingly to the hope we profess, for he who promised is faithful. . . . Let us not give up meeting together, as some are in the habit of doing, but let us encourage one another—and all the more as you see the Day approaching" (Heb. 10:23, 25).

For those first-century believers, there were no "See you next week" farewells, or the expectation for any member to "go it alone." The growing number of disciples gave personal attention to the needs of each other in the context of everyday living. No one was forgotten. They put into action the mandate to love one another!

* * * * * * * * * *

The television was blaring as Diane opened the front door. In front of the set Chuck was sleeping soundly. Diane turned off the television, which brought Chuck out of his sleep.

"Diane, you just got home?"

"Just walked in the door," answered Diane. "Sweetheart, you really missed a good meeting."

Chuck sat up, took off his glasses, and rubbed his eyes.

"And what new evangelism techniques did you learn?"

"Chuck, it wasn't like that."

"Oh, come on, Diane, admit it. You learned three new methods for buttonholing people for Jesus. In fact, your purse is probably packed with new 'miracle tracts' guaranteed to make people instant Christians."

Diane was exasperated. "Chuck, believe me. We didn't even talk about methods of witnessing. What we studied

22

about was the Early Church and their strategy for disciple-making."

Chuck stood up. "Diane, can't you see what Pastor Austin's doing? He's setting you up. And next week you will learn what evangelism methods were used by the Early Church—and how we can use them today. Right?"

"You're probably right. But maybe we should learn to use their methods. After all, didn't they turn their world upside down?" Diane gave Chuck a parting smile and headed for the bedroom.

"But, Diane . . ."

It was too late. She was gone and the discussion was over.

2

How New Disciples Are Made
The *Oikos* Factor

"Joshua, a Jewish merchant from Rome, walked briskly along the cobblestone road. He knew, as he passed more and more people, that he was getting closer. He had heard much and thought often about the city of David; a thought shared by every Jew throughout the Roman world. Forty years earlier Herod the Great had begun a major restoring project in Jerusalem to return it to its former grandeur. Not since the time of King Solomon had such palaces, citadels, amphitheaters, viaducts, and public monuments been built. So magnificent were these buildings begun by Herod that some were still being completed. Joshua had heard that visitors were overwhelmed by the city's splendor."

Chuck restlessly changed position. Pastor Austin was doing another of his fictional, quasibiblical narratives and Chuck wasn't interested.

"The winding road made its way over a hill of gnarled olive trees. Joshua's pulse quickened, his pace increased. As a Jewish merchant, he had 'officially' made this trip for business reasons. But secretly Joshua had always longed for a reason to take the several-week journey from Rome to Jerusalem to see the city of his dreams. Nearing the top of the last hill, he no longer noticed or nodded to travelers passing on the road. He was sure that on the other side of the hill

. . . He broke into a run, sandals clapping against the cobblestones.

"Then, he saw it. He gazed, transfixed. Joshua could not believe he was actually there. Across the valley, sat among the surrounding hills, was Jerusalem . . . 'the perfection of beauty' in the words of Lamentations, 'the joy of all the world.'"

Why, Chuck wondered, had he let Diane talk him into coming to this disciple-making class?

Why, Chuck wondered, had he let Diane talk him into coming to the second session of Pastor Austin's seminar on "Disciple-making: The Master's Plan"? Was it because she had been so insistent? Or was it because, as a committed Christian, he carried guilt feelings about his lack of fruitfulness as a witness for his Lord?

"As Joshua approached the city, he could see how the massive stone wall that surrounded it had been damaged, repaired, and enlarged over the centuries. At intervals along the wall were massive gateways where people streamed in and out of the city. Just inside each gate was a customs station where publicans collected taxes on all goods entering and leaving the city. Joshua explained his mission to the gatekeepers and was told to report to the customs center near the Temple where an officer would explain the regulations.

"Once inside the city, Joshua faced a bewildering maze of dusty, winding streets and alleyways. As he pushed his way through the crowds, slowly making his way toward the Temple, his senses were assaulted by the sounds of voices raised in bartering or in song, the braying of donkeys, odors of cooking bread, and the bleating of sheep soon to be sacrificed. In the excitement, Joshua nearly forgot to ask directions to his brother-in-law Benjamin's house where he would be staying while in Jerusalem."

Chuck glanced at Diane. She was far away—with Pastor Austin in first-century Jerusalem. Chuck discreetly checked his watch. When would Pastor Austin get to his point? Who cares about some imaginary Jewish merchant from the first century?

"The next day Joshua spent as a tourist walking through the city. Since it was the holiday feast of Pentecost, most merchants were not doing business. As Joshua entered the marketplace, he noticed a gathering on the far side of the court. It seemed to be a political meeting or a public debate.

"Walking closer, Joshua saw a large, bearded man standing above the crowd, speaking to them. Suddenly Joshua's heart jumped. He couldn't believe what he was hearing. The Jewish man was speaking in perfect and fluent Latin, a language Joshua had not heard since he left the Roman ship on the coast of Israel. He listened.

"The man speaking called himself Peter. He spoke of

strange but fascinating things—of the Messiah, foretold by the prophets, and that this Messiah had already come. In fact, Peter claimed that he had actually been with the Messiah only days before! His message filled Joshua with a strange sense of intrigue. It was unthinkable that the Messiah had actually come. Everyone would know! Yet the story this man told sounded reasonable and compelling. Could the long-awaited Messiah actually have come?

"Later that day Joshua responded to Peter's message about the risen Christ and His love. Joshua and 3,000 others were baptized. He hurried home to tell Benjamin, his brother-in-law, and his family of this exciting new dimension to the Jewish faith. That night as Joshua, overflowing with joy, shared the events of the day, Benjamin, Benjamin's wife Miriam, and their whole family decided to follow Jesus, the Messiah.

"In order to learn more about his new faith, Joshua stayed in Jerusalem longer than he originally planned. He, Benjamin, and Miriam joined other believers as 'they devoted themselves to the apostles' teaching and to the fellowship, to the breaking of bread and to prayer' (Acts 2:42).

"Joshua wrote home to his wife, Ruth, and the children to explain his delay. He told them of his new faith, and sent the letter by Ananiah, a friend in Rome who was visiting Jerusalem and who had become a disciple at Pentecost.

"When Joshua returned to Rome, his family became disciples of Jesus the Messiah. Joshua began sharing the apostles' teaching with his family and with Ananiah. Soon Ananiah's family and servants also came to the Lord.

"Meanwhile, Joshua returned to his import-export business. He gathered his employees around to tell them of this new faith. Many of them believed and asked Joshua to help them share the Good News with their families.

"Whether he knew it or not, Joshua was part of a process of making disciples that would eventually make the

Christian movement the most widespread faith and force on earth. And a key element in that process was the communication of God's love through an established network of social relationships, which the Greek New Testament calls *oikos*."

Almost imperceptibly Chuck shook his head. Doesn't Pastor Austin realize that we don't live in the first century? What may have worked then doesn't necessarily work today!

* * * * * * * * * *

Chuck's question of the applicability of 2,000-year-old principles deserves an answer. But first let's examine the meaning of the new word *oikos* introduced by Pastor Austin.

The word *oikos* is the Greek word for "household." In the Graeco-Roman culture *oikos* described not only the immediate family in the house but also included servants, servants' families, friends, and even business associates. "An oikos was one's sphere of influence, the social system composed of those related to each other through common kinship ties, tasks, and territory."[1]

The Household and the Old Testament

The Old Testament pictures the household as including several generations in a family. In the book *Anthology of the Old Testament,* Hans Walter Wolff observes, "A household usually contained four generations, including men, married women, unmarried daughters, slaves of both sexes, persons without citizenship, and 'sojourners,' or resident foreign workers."[2] Old Testament scripture confirms again and again the significance and uniqueness of the household and the family. God's original promise to Abraham included the provision that through him ". . . all families of the earth [shall] be blessed" (Gen. 12:3, KJV).

28

Oikos and the New Testament

God continues to focus on the household (friends, extended family, associates) in the New Testament in His plans for communicating to mankind. The Gospels, Acts, and the Epistles show that the bridges of *oikos* were used regularly as a means to spread the Good News. After healing a demon-possessed man, Jesus told him, "Go home to your family *[oikos]* and tell them how much the Lord has done for you, and how he has had mercy on you" (Mark 5:19).

After Zacchaeus was converted, Jesus said to him, "Today salvation has come to this house *[oikos]*" (Luke 19:9).

When Jesus healed the son of a royal official, "He and all his household *[oikos]* believed" (John 4:53).

Levi followed Jesus, and invited his fellow tax collectors —his *oikos*—to come to dinner, and as a result many followed Christ (see Mark 2:14-15).

The apostle Peter came to Christ because of someone in his *oikos*: "The first thing Andrew did was to find his brother Simon and tell him, 'We have found the Messiah'" (John 1:41). Nathanael came to Christ because his friend Philip "found Nathanael and told him, 'We have found the one Moses wrote about in the Law. . . . '" (John 1:45).

Following Christ's resurrection and ascension, it was this same pattern of the gospel moving through the *oikos* that caused the Early Church to flourish. Church historian Kenneth Scott Latourette has observed that "the primary change agents in the spread of faith . . . were the men and women who earned their livelihood in some purely secular manner, and spoke of their faith to those whom they met in this natural fashion."[3]

Paul and his companions shared Christ with a businesswoman named Lydia, outside the city of Philippi. The Bible records that she responded to their message and that she and the members of her household were baptized (see Acts 16:15).

Shortly thereafter, Paul and Silas were thrown into jail. As they were praying and singing hymns, an earthquake freed all the prisoners of their chains. Rather than face death because of the escaped prisoners, the jailer prepared to kill himself. But Paul assured him they were still there and the jailer asked, "'Men, what must I do to be saved?' They replied, 'Believe in the Lord Jesus, and you will be saved—you and your household.' Then they spoke the word of the Lord to him and to all the others in his house *[oikos]* . . . Then immediately he and all his family were baptized . . . and the whole family was filled with joy, because they had come to believe in God" (Acts 16:30-34).

In the book *Bridges of God,* McGavran re-creates a probable scene from biblical times:

"Some Jewish woman in Antioch may have said to Paul: 'I have a brother in Iconium. He has, for many years, longed for the coming of the Messiah. How I wish it were possible for him to hear you! He has a large house and has prospered in business. He would give you a genuine welcome. Do let me send him word.'

"Wherever he went, Paul must have had someone's brother-in-law or second cousin or aunt or uncle to look up. He could approach such a person with a message: 'Simon sends his greetings, and says to tell you the family is well. He hopes you and your household are well, and he said that you might like to hear the message we bear, that the Messiah has come and brought a new way of life.' Think of the great receptivity such contacts would have produced! It is, to us, an inescapable inference that Paul at Antioch must have known of many such relatives and must have realized their enormous importance in the extension of the faith."[4]

Paul was not the only one spreading the gospel. Thousands of Christians were telling friends and relatives in their *oikos* about Jesus.

* * * * * * * * * *

Chuck could wait no longer. He raised his hand. "But, Pastor, what basis do we have for assuming that this *oikos* concept works today?"

"But, Pastor, what basis do we have for assuming that this *oikos* concept works today?"

Diane was a little embarrassed by Chuck's bluntness, but Pastor Austin didn't seem to mind the question. "Good question, Chuck. I think the best way to answer that would be to take a few minutes and share some of the various ways some of us have come to Christ and to this church. Who'll be first?"

An older woman in the front row raised her hand. Standing, she told the group how she was now in the church because of a friend from church who lived in her mobile home park. This friend invited her to attend a revival at the church. She came to the meetings and made a Christian commitment. Even though her friend had since passed away, she has continued as an active Christian and member of the church.

A younger woman, about 25, told how she had come to Christ through her Christian parents. When she moved to this town to take a job, she began looking for a church. A friend of hers at work was attending this church, so it was a natural step into the church after she had visited a few times.

A middle-aged man then told how one of his cousins, who lived in town, had introduced him and the family to Christ and this church.

"Chuck, does that answer your question?"

"Yeah. I'd say that answers it." Chuck turned to Diane, who gave him an "I told you so" smile.

* * * * * * * * * *

The Importance of *Oikos* Today

Webs of *common kinship* (the larger family), *common friendship* (friends and neighbors), and *common associates* (special interests, work relationships, and recreation) are still the paths most people follow in becoming Christians today.

Research conducted by the Institute of American Church Growth of Pasadena, Calif., on why people have come to Christ and the Church, provides astonishing support on the *oikos* process at work today.[5] Over 17,000 laypeople have been asked the question: "What or who was responsible for your coming to Christ and your church?" One of the following responses was usually given: (1) a *special need* brought them to Christ and the church; (2) they just *walked in;* (3) the *pastor;* (4) *visitation;* (5) the *Sunday School;* (6) *evangelistic crusade* (or *television program*); (7) the church *program* attracted them; (8) finally, many responded *friend/relative.*

In seven of the eight categories, the percentage of respondents was small, but in the eighth more than three-fourths of the people said they came to Christ and the church because of a friend/relative.

The majority of people today can trace their "spiritual roots" directly to a friend or a relative as the major reason they are in Christ and their church. (Do some research in your own church to see if this holds true.)

The following are actual examples of how people come to Christ and the church today.

In the Grove City, Ohio, Nazarene Church an evangelism family tree has grown up through the *oikos* principle. It began as a result of a young couple coming to Christ and the church, who have since been responsible (either directly or indirectly) for bringing 35 other adults (plus 32 children) to Christ and the church.

A Kansas City First Church member won one of his friends to the Lord. This opened up four webs that ultimately brought 14 people to the church.

In Albion, Pa., a woman received an invitation to the Nazarene church from one of its members. This began a web that resulted in 29 people (of which 19 are adults) becoming a part of the church.

The centuries-old concept of *oikos*, or webs, continues to be the bridge over which the Good News of God's love travels naturally.

Why *Oikos* Is Effective

Why do people respond so positively to the gospel as it travels through these "webs" of relationships?

1. *Oikos Relationships Provide a Natural Network for Sharing the Good News of God's Redemptive Love.* The new Christian, who has discovered the genuine joy of experiencing God's saving grace, is naturally eager to tell others. He wants to share this new freedom and joy with the *oikos* of friends, relatives, and associates—people who mean the most to him.

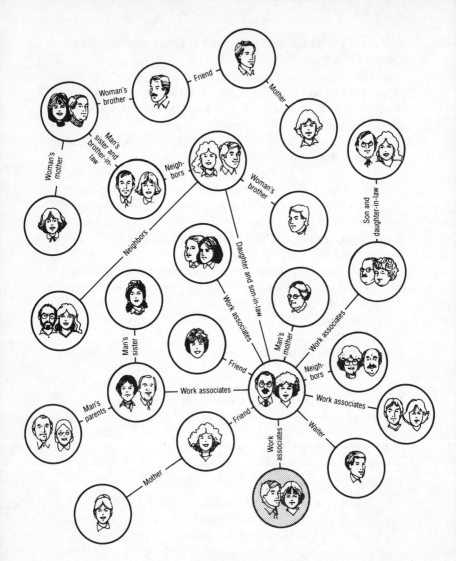

Grove City, Ohio
Church of the Nazarene

34

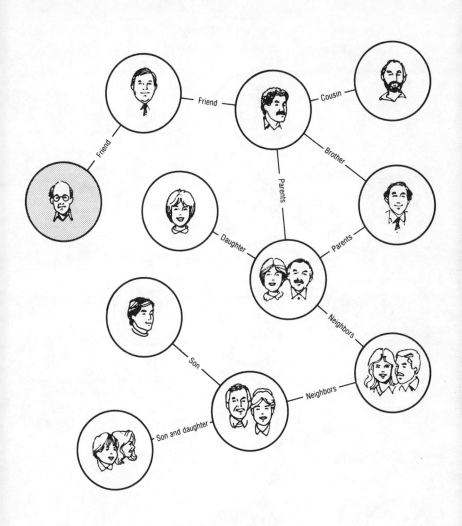

Kansas City, Missouri
First Church of the Nazarene

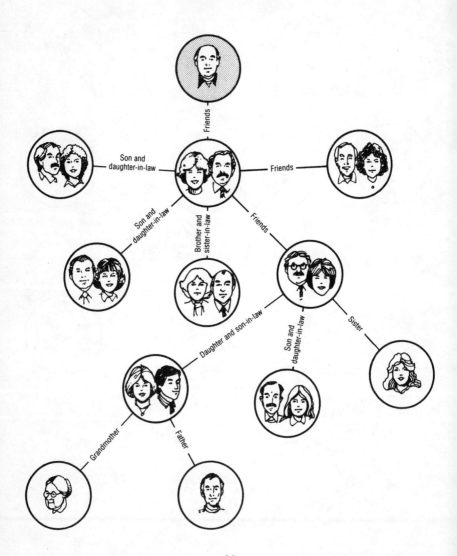

36

"I believe Nancy and Susan are good examples of how the *oikos* principle has worked in our church," Pastor Austin smiled at two young women in the second row. "Susan, would you mind sharing with the group how you and Nancy became disciples?"

"Sure," said Susan. "Nancy and I had been roommates for a little over a year. We got along well together and enjoyed each other's company. Neither of us was a Christian, so it came as quite a shock to me one day when she came home and started talking about having committed her life to Jesus Christ."

2. *Oikos Members Are Receptive.* When God's love is discussed with an *oikos* member, that person is usually open and receptive since he is listening to the experience of someone known and trusted.

"I remember," continued Susan, "when Nancy began explaining her new attitudes and belief, I was really interested. She still seemed to be normal; I mean, she hadn't all of a sudden freaked out or anything." Susan laughed and looked at Nancy. "And talking with her in our apartment, I felt comfortable asking questions and discussing her new ideas and faith."

3. *Oikos Relationships Allow for a Natural Sharing of God's Love.* Relationships with *oikos* members, by their very nature, are easy and natural, whether on a social outing or in the comfort of a living room. And the Christian life-style demonstrates Christ's love in a variety of places, times, and situations.

"Although I was interested, I needed time to think about what it all meant," said Susan. "I had a lot of preconceived notions about what a Christian was and did, and I needed some time to see what Nancy's new commitment really meant. As days and months went by, I saw some significant changes in Nancy, and being around her and seeing what her faith meant to her had an important effect on my thinking."

4. *Oikos Relationships Provide Natural Support When the Web Member Comes to Christ.* Since at least one Christian—the original web member—is close to the new convert and eager to see growth in his new life, new Christians are not left alone. There is someone to love, care for, and nurture them.

"After three months, I began attending church with Nancy," Susan recalled. "Before long I decided to commit my life to Christ. As a young Christian it has meant a great deal to have Nancy's loving support helping me grow as a disciple."

5. *Oikos Relationships Result in the Effective Assimilation of New Converts into the Church.* It is natural for the new Christian to attend church where a friend or family member belongs. Because of this "bridge," the new Christian can more easily become associated with other Christians in a Sunday School class or fellowship group and can begin to build new relationships and friendships within the Body.

"I really feel at home in this church. Although at first it was 'Nancy's church.' It soon became my church, too. I joined the Sunday School class where Nancy was a member and met many new friends. The social activities sponsored by the church also helped me feel part of the group."

6. *Oikos Relationships Tend to Win Entire Families.* When one or two people in a family come to Christ and the church, it is often the beginning of a process that results in the entire family becoming new disciples. As the entire family grows together in Christ, the family unit is strengthened. On the other hand, if the entire family is not reached, conflict and fragmentation may result. An immediate emphasis should be

placed on identifying and reaching others in a family once one member has made a Christian commitment.

"After I made a commitment to Christ and joined this church," Susan concluded, "I immediately told my mother, brother, and sister-in-law of the exciting new discovery I had made. I'm hoping they, too, will soon discover the joy of being a Christian. Anyway, I'm praying for them."

7. *Oikos Relationships Provide a Constantly Enlarging Source of New Contacts.* Each new person reached for Christ and the church has his own group of relatives, friends, and associates who are candidates for the Good News. Research shows that, on the average, each new Christian has 12 people in his *oikos* who are non-Christians. (Older Christians often have less; the average in most churches is about eight.) The process of identifying receptive people and reaching out is never completed, because with each conversion there are new contacts and opportunities.

Throughout the 2,000-year history of the Church, God has richly blessed its growth through webs of *oikos* relationships.[6] The *oikos* concept is timely, yet timeless. It is planned, yet not contrived. It is founded on solid church growth research, experience, and principles found throughout Scripture. It is the way churches have grown and continue to grow.

* * * * * * * * *

After the session Chuck cornered Pastor Austin with another question. "Wouldn't the gospel have spread faster," Chuck asked, "if the Early Church had been able to use modern media—like radio and television?"

Pastor Austin smiled and shook his head. "No, Chuck, I don't think so. The first-century church had a better medium for communicating God's love."

"Wouldn't the gospel have spread faster if the Early Church had had modern media?" Chuck wondered aloud.

"And what was that?"

"Well, it was what we talked about tonight . . . the *oikos* network. And, Chuck, it's still the best medium."

3

Incorporation— the Entry Essential for Making Disciples

"Isn't that Mike Jensen sitting over there?" Diane whispered, not wanting to disturb the people around them who were listening attentively to Pastor Austin announce a special church function.

Pastor Austin was announcing a special church function.

Chuck looked in the direction Diane had indicated and was surprised to see Mike, an acquaintance of his. "It is! I didn't see him come in."

"Let's be sure and introduce him to Bob and Tim," Diane said.

"Maybe we shouldn't crowd him. Let's give him time to get used to the church."

But Diane saw right through Chuck's reluctance. "Introducing him to a few people isn't going to frighten him away. Besides, getting acquainted with several people is a good way to get used to the church."

Diane was right, as usual, and Chuck knew it. And so after the service was over Chuck and Diane worked their way through the worshipers and exited through the side door. They caught up with Mike just as he was going through the front door.

"Mike, I haven't seen you in quite a while," Chuck said.

"Hello, Chuck. Hi, Diane. I didn't know you two came to this church."

Just then Tim was walking by, so Chuck said, "It's so good to have you in church, Mike. Here, let me introduce you to Tim . . ."

That morning they introduced Mike to four families in the church, not fully realizing the importance of this action.

* * * * * * * * * *

INCORPORATION—The process of involving new contacts with church people, programs, and facilities so they feel socially comfortable in the church environment.

Incorporation may well be the most crucial aspect of making disciples. This is true because it takes place at the

42

front end of the evangelism process. Unless incorporation is effective, the Good News will not have opportunity to impact people. Even though personal evangelism teams secure a decision in the home of new contacts, the disciple-making process is likely to fail unless the new believers are socially incorporated into the fellowship of the church.

Put yourself in the shoes of visitors to your church. When they walk into the vestibule they are unfamiliar with the building and unacquainted with anyone. That makes for significant social discomfort. A church that recognizes this and organizes to overcome it will be much more effective in making disciples.

In order to succeed at the job of incorporating new people it is helpful to understand what is involved in incorporation. There are at least four factors to be considered.

1. *Adequate Acquaintance.* Visitors need to meet enough people in the church so they can stop and visit with two or three persons following each service. Even though they only talk about the weather, it is a bridge to people and ultimately to friendships.

2. *Familiarity with the Setting and Procedure.* Most church members are so accustomed to the church building that they are unable to understand the uneasiness a visitor feels just because of the strange surroundings. In time the discomfort will disappear, but effort should be put forth to prevent it from being a negative factor in evangelism.

Worship customs pose a similar threat to visitors. They are uncertain of the extent to which they are to participate in the acts of worship. Practices that might make visitors feel ill at ease need to be directed in ways that create understanding.

3. *A Sense of Acceptance.* There needs to be an interaction between members and visitors that will cause the new people to feel accepted. Members can be trained in ways to make their acceptance obvious. Sincere thoughtfulness and

43

INCORPORATION/ASSIMILATION SCALE

INCORPORATION (Social)	−10	Knows nothing of a particular church
	−9	Aware of church but knows no one in the church
	−8	Knows someone in the church
	−7	Has a personal friend in the church
	−6	Has two or more friends in the church
	−5	Has been involved in a social event related to the church
	−4	Has visited the church
	−3	Is involved in a church activity, for example, Bible study, recreational group
	−2	Attends church frequently
	−1	Familiarity with setting and worship style
	0	Feels sense of belonging and social comfort
ASSIMILATION (Psychological)	+1	Conversion
	+2	Regular attendance
	+3	Baptism
	+4	Developing friendships
	+5	Church membership
	+6	Sanctification
	+7	Accepts responsibility
	+8	Trusted by membership

genuine consideration are basic to helping visitors feel accepted.

4. *Developing Friendships.* People will not be incorporated until they begin to develop some friendships. Visitors aren't looking for a friendly church. They are looking for a friend. A strong handshake and a warm invitation to come again must be backed by genuine caring. Friendliness that

holds no potential for friendship is a hollow misrepresentation. Visitors sense this and are unlikely to keep returning unless some genuine friendships are available to them.

Hindrances to Incorporation

There are three main hindrances to incorporating new people into the fellowship of the church.

1. *Lack of Awareness.* Most church members do not realize that new people need to be socially incorporated. Perhaps the spiritual aspect of the church causes members to overlook the socially related factors of the fellowship. But when we talk about social incorporation we are talking about evangelism. We may dismiss it as just a social program, but if we do, we will allow the souls of multiplied numbers of people to slip through our fingers. Social relationships are the connecting links that carry the good news of salvation.

2. *Lack of Healthy Group Life.* In many churches the groups are either closed or limited in number and/or kind. The most common problem is closed groups. This is an exclusive condition and drives new people away in disappointment rather than drawing them into the life of the church. A limited number of groups is also a negative factor. Groups can only contain a limited number of people. When the groups of a church are full, incorporation will be difficult to accomplish. It is best for a church to have several groups with sufficient variety to attract and incorporate different kinds of people.

3. *Lack of Organization.* Without organization incorporation will not happen—at least not regularly. There must be intentionality in our efforts to incorporate new people.

Effective Incorporation

How do we insure that new contacts become acquainted with the life of the congregation, that they develop a sense of acceptance and belonging?

45

The question of incorporation is crucial. A strategy for successful incorporation of new people is a major part of any church's commitment to making disciples. A church-centered approach to incorporation rightly assumes the centrality of the church in this process.

Here are five steps to seeing an effective incorporation strategy become a reality in your church.

1. *Build an "Incorporation Consciousness."* A church with an incorporation consciousness is one where people go out of their way to greet newcomers and get to know them; where they do everything possible to make people feel welcome and an important part of the church. In most churches, however, an "incorporation consciousness" does not naturally occur. And while many congregations like to think of themselves as a "friendly church," a first-time visitor might have a quite different impression. Often smaller groups in a church, without realizing it, actually exclude and even isolate newcomers. A conscious and continuous effort must be made, therefore, to encourage laypeople and groups in the church to be open to outsiders.

Building an incorporation consciousness is not difficult. But it requires a high priority on the part of church leaders, officers, and members. Sunday School class sessions, small-group meetings, worship services, and midweek prayer meetings should frequently stress to each layperson the importance of being open and caring to the newcomer.

2. *Develop an Incorporation Structure.* More and more churches, seeing the need for a formal concern for the incorporation of new people, are establishing a special committee. Here are some suggestions for organizing a system for incorporation in your church:

- Establish a "new contact tracking committee" of laypeople exclusively concerned with overseeing the first few months of the new contact's life in the fellowship.

The committee keeps accurate records and updated information on every new contact. It provides information to each class or small group regarding the incorporation activities in which the person has been involved.

- Appoint a person in each Sunday School class and small group in the church to be responsible for the incorporation of new people. Such a person is responsible to see that new people are introduced to others in the group, and that the class or group is open to accept them.

- Research previous incorporation results. Analyze the present level of involvement of church members who have joined the church in the last two years. How many are now active church members, and how many have dropped out? Studying the patterns of incorporation gives unique insights into present strengths and weaknesses.

3. *Provide Friendship-Building Opportunities.* As we have seen, the number of close friends a new contact develops in the church has a direct influence on whether he continues in the fellowship. If, after six months, the new contact can identify few or no close friends in the church, the chances are extremely high that the person will soon drop out. But if the new contact has a growing number of close friends who are active in the church, it will be very unusual for that person to drop out. The "friendship factor," research tells us, is the most important element in whether a person remains active in a local church, or drops out.[1] This is true even though a person has had a genuine personal conversion to Christ and has made the necessary adjustments to a Christian life-style.

What does this mean for your church?

One implication is that church groups should provide opportunities for building friendships with new people. Organize activities that are just plain fun! Activities that strengthen personal ties in the fellowship. Be sure that both members and new contacts attend. The event should not be just to entertain the same old gang.

An effective incorporation strategy will help new people build additional relationships beyond the friend/relative originally responsible for bringing the person to the church. You will know your incorporation strategy is working when you see new contacts become Christians and remain active even when the original friend or relative moves to another city or goes on to be with the Lord.

4. *Structure Need-Meeting Ministries.* A fourth step toward an effective incorporation strategy for new people centers on the unique needs that these people bring to the church—personal, spiritual, marital, occupational, relational. Life is full of problems. A church concerned with seeing people grow and mature in the Christian life should have ministries that directly respond to the needs of people.

Starting new groups is an excellent way to provide such support. Groups or classes may be topically oriented and deal with certain areas of concern to members. A list of such need-meeting classes might look like this:

Personal

—How to reduce weight
—Stop-smoking seminars
—Coping with stress
—Feeling good about yourself
—Self-discipline—why and how

Spiritual

—What the Bible says about _____
—Daily Bible study—why and how
—Prayer: Is anyone listening?

Marital

—Communicating with your spouse
—Your marriage: the first 100 days
—New parents class
—Children and drugs

Occupational

—Dealing with job-related anxiety
—Reentering the job market
—Changing jobs

Relational

—Learning to listen
—How to deepen your friendships
—Dating and the Christian
—Coping with in-laws

Obviously there are many others. And the ministries provided will vary according to age, marital status, personal interests, particular needs. The best way to identify appropriate groups or topics is to form an ad hoc committee responsible for identifying various areas of need to which the church can respond. If your Great Commission conscience is beginning to develop, you will see that such need-meeting ministries can provide ideal opportunities to introduce yet-to-be-reached extended family members to the church and its people.

5. *Monitor Incorporation Results.* A key and ongoing part of effective incorporation involves monitoring new contacts' involvement in the church. Systematically observing worship attendance, Sunday School attendance, and involvement in small-group meetings provides important clues as to the new person's feeling of satisfaction with his church life. Closely monitor the involvement levels of each new person for the first several months of life in the fellowship. And respond immediately at the first sign of problems.

Incorporation does not take the place of the Word, the

conviction of the Holy Spirit, or the necessity of repentance and conversion. It has its *own* place. Incorporation is pre-evangelism in the truest sense. For without incorporation true evangelism—making disciples—will seldom get the chance to occur. How, indeed, can people "believe in the one of whom they have not heard?" (Rom. 10:14).

4

Key Principles of Disciple-making

The bright morning sun had little effect on Chuck as he sat sipping his breakfast coffee. He had slept badly, tossing and turning most of the night.

"What's wrong, sweetheart?" asked Diane.

"I just can't do it!"

"Can't do what?"

"I just can't do it!"

51

"Diane, I just don't think I can share my faith. And I know that I should! I lay awake most of the night thinking about it."

"But, Chuck, why do you feel that way?"

"Well, that's what I've been wrestling with. I think it's because I feel inadequate. I mean, who am I to explain the gospel to people? I've never even been to seminary!"

"But, Chuck, none of the apostles ever went to seminary. And they did pretty well at sharing their faith!"

"Yeah, but they were apostles. Besides, I'm not good enough. You know I'm not, Diane."

"Chuck, stop putting yourself down. Did you ever think what would have happened if the first Christians had waited until they were perfect before sharing their faith? The church would have died right in the first century."

Chuck nodded. "I never thought of that. But, Diane, who would be interested in my witness?"

"What do you mean?"

"Well, you know how people are today. They're only interested in money . . . and things . . . and having a good time. No one's interested in the church—or my faith."

Diane placed her hand over his.

"Chuck, you believe that your relationship to Jesus Christ makes a difference in your life."

"Well, sure, I wouldn't be a Christian if I didn't. Diane, that's what bothers me most. I would like to share my faith—if I could!"

* * * * * * * * *

"God So Loved the World . . ."

God's unswerving purpose is the discipling of mankind. He calls His Church and each of His disciples to a deliberate commitment to this. As we saw in the first chapter, this is the priority of Christ and the command to His Church.

Most Christians and churches believe this. The problem comes when church leaders and laypeople try to translate this "call to arms" into specific marching orders. "What can we as a church, or as individuals, really do that is significant? And how do we do it?" Indeed, this shortage of practical, "do-able" guidelines for effective church evangelism is one of the greatest frustrations in the church today. "Go and make disciples . . . fine, but how?"

It's for this reason that we suggest an approach to disciple-making in and through the local church. The approach is not a program but a process, a process that builds on the natural "webs" of relationships that exist in every church. It is a process that can be a rewarding, fruitful experience for each participating church member. We call it *The Master's Plan!*

The Master's Plan merges New Testament principles and modern church growth insights to help you and your church respond more effectively to Christ's Great Commission where He has placed you.

The Master's Plan is a strategy of disciple-making to help lay church members identify and reach the people in their webs, or *oikos,* for Christ and the Church. *The Master's Plan* is a fulfilling, satisfying life-style for all church members. It is one of the most enjoyable experiences a Christian will have in his lifetime—guaranteed!

The Master's Plan builds on the scriptural insight that the Christian message travels best over natural bridges of friendships and relationships *(oikos)*. It is based on the conviction that God wants lost humanity found. The bottom line in effective evangelism is whether people are won to Christ and the church grows. The motivation behind a concern for effective disciple-making is the conviction that God desires His church to proclaim the gospel and make disciples. *The Master's Plan,* when incorporated and practiced in the local church, is an intentional and effective way to see this happen.

Principles of *The Master's Plan*

What are the cornerstones of this approach to disciple-making in the local church? There are nine key principles in *The Master's Plan* disciple-making strategy. Here is a brief statement of each.

Principle No. 1—*Disciple-making is most effective when it is an intentional response by the local church to the Great Commission.*

Intentionality in evangelism is the church's response to Christ's command to make disciples. It is an act of obedience, an acknowledgment of His Lordship. It means that: (1) disciple-making becomes part of the priorities and goals of the church; (2) the church regularly measures itself against the yardstick of the numbers of new disciples it produces; (3) the church makes a commitment to disciple-making and sticks with it; (4) the purpose and activities of groups within the church include specific and intentional steps to bring new disciples continually into the local body of believers.

Such intentional evangelism does not happen automatically. In fact, a church often grows "inward" over time, becoming more concerned with its own survival and less concerned with its call to multiply itself.

Intentionality in outreach means doing something. But it doesn't mean doing just anything. Effective evangelism requires insight and study as to the best and most productive intentional efforts.

Effective disciple-making combines intentional growth principles with an "evangelistic mix" that fits the local church's unique situation.

Principle No. 2—*Disciple-making is most effective when focused on the "oikos" (natural networks) of existing Christians.*

As discussed in Chapter 2, webs of common kinship (the larger family), common friendship (friends, neighbors), and common associates (special interests, work relationships, recreation), are the means by which most people become Christians.

Here are eight important reasons why identifying and using natural networks of relationships should be the foundation for the outreach strategy of every church:

1. It is the natural way churches grow;
2. It is the most cost-effective way to reach new people;
3. It is the most fruitful way to win new people;
4. It provides a constantly enlarging source of new contacts;
5. It brings the greatest satisfaction to participating members;
6. It results in the most effective assimilation of new members;
7. It tends to win entire families;
8. It uses existing relationships.

Principle No. 3—*Disciple-making is most effective when based on, and permeated with, love and caring.*

"My comand is this: Love each other as I have loved you. Greater love has no one than this, that one lay down his life for his friends." (John 15:12-13).

Caring for people is a key distinctive and quality of effective disciple-making . . . a genuine expression of God's unconditional love. God has seen fit to communicate His love to non-Christians through His representatives. "The person who loves God loves his brother also" (see 1 John 4:21).

The translation of Christ's "love" into tangible, specific action is the process of "caring." Caring is spending time with persons, building stronger and closer relationships, helping in times of need. "We know that we have passed from death to life, because we love our brothers. . . . Dear children, let us not love with words or tongue but with actions and in truth" (1 John 3:14, 18).

"I have called you friends, for everything that I learned from my Father I have made known to you. You did not choose me, but I chose you to go and bear fruit—fruit that will last. . . . This is my command: Love each other" (John 15:15-17).

Principle No. 4—*Disciple-making is most effective when each Christian has a part in responding to the Great Commission.*

Any church member who can identify an unchurched friend, relative, neighbor, or associate can be a disciple-maker. Since an average church member has from 4 to 12 unchurched friends/relatives, a church of 100 members would have an average of 8 unchurched friends/relatives per member. The prospect list of potential disciples would be 800 of the most receptive people anywhere in that community. Making disciples becomes the concern of *each* member as he communicates God's love to these people.

This widespread lay participation in disciple-making not only contributes to enlarged church outreach, but also results in increased Christian maturity among participating church members and throughout the spiritual life of the Body. Individual Christians actively involved in the Great Commission feel, perhaps for the first time, that they are making a significant contribution to the cause of Christ. Being part of such a cause gives an important sense of spiritual self-worth.

Often we assume that spiritual growth occurs only in the context of daily prayer, regular Bible study, and frequent participation in Sunday School and church. Certainly all these are important, but "Christlikeness" can hardly be an achievable goal if there is no participation in the basic reason for Christ's mission.

Christ said it best: "Unless a kernel of wheat falls to the ground and dies, it remains only a single seed. But if it dies, it produces many seeds. The man who loves his life will lose it, while the man who hates his life in this world will keep it for eternal life" (John 12:24-25).

Being part of productive disciple-making is great spiritual therapy! It can spark the most weary Christians and churches into a new flame.

Principle No. 5—*Disciple-making is most effective when it is a "team effort."*

God hasn't planned for us to be isolated. He has given us a community of brothers and sisters. A community whose whole is greater than the sum of its parts.

Why is a "team effort" more productive for disciple-making than any one individual's effort?

Each member has been given different gifts to build up the Body (see Eph. 4:16). Peter in 1 Pet. 4:10 notes that each Christian has been given a gift. Paul says, "Now about spiritual gifts, brothers, I do not want you to be ignorant" (1 Cor. 12:1). Effective disciple-making, therefore, means using your own gift, then supplementing yours with other gifts in a team effort to build the Body.

A second reason why a team effort will be more effective in disciple-making is that the more and varied the contacts a non-Christian has with the Body, the more completely that person will see Christ.

A third reason why a team effort is more productive is that on a practical level, these non-Christians *have to* make new Christian friends in the church or they won't stay! Research indicates that in most cases, the new Christians who soon "drop out" of active church involvement never made new friends in that church. Evangelism that does not include this important friendship factor will result in much loss of labor.[1]

Principle No. 6—*Disciple-making is most effective when it is church-centered.*

The more distant evangelism is from the local church, the

less "fruit" remains; the closer evangelism is to the local church, the more "fruit" remains. Disciple-making revolves around the local church. It is energized through the local church. The results accrue to the local church. The process of disciple-making has the church at the center of the evangelistic focus and builds on the vast resources available through the Body.

One of the traditional forces in the Church of the Nazarene is the practice of local churches conducting annual revivals. Not only are these revivals times when Christian people are renewed in the faith, but they are also opportunities for new people to be converted. Revivals are an especially effective means by which Christians can expose the members of their webs of influence to the gospel. Usually these special services are followed by an opportunity for a public expression of faith. Revival meetings have been perennial harvesttimes in Nazarene churches.

While the church's unique role in *The Master's Plan* is examined in detail in Chapters 8 and 9, the following functions of the church are central to effective disciple-making:

- The church initiates disciple-making through an intentional strategy;
- The church trains its members in effective disciple-making;
- The church coordinates the resources of the Body for effective disciple-making;
- The church creates programs and ministries for effective disciple-making;
- The church structures accountability into disciple-making.

Principle No. 7—*Disciple-making is most effective when unique needs and individual differences are recognized and celebrated.*

"I have become all things to all men so that by all possible means I might save some. I do all this for the sake of the gospel" (1 Cor. 9:22-23).

People come to Christ in many different ways, for many different reasons. And for Christ to be considered as a viable alternative in anyone's life, the gospel must be presented in ways that speak to those unique needs.

Effective disciple-making recognizes the unique differences of the friends and relatives in each member's web *(oikos)*. The following questions help clarify some of the differences among non-Christians in a person's *oikos* that have an effect on how God's love should be communicated:

- What is the level and depth of my relationship with this person?
- What other Christians/church members does he know well?
- What are this person's understandings of Christianity? What are the misunderstandings?
- How receptive is the person to becoming a Christian?
- Would this person feel comfortable in our church (regarding such factors as age, marital status, race, ethnicity, socioeconomic status, common interest)?

A study of the gospel reveals that Christ himself was a powerful demonstration of meeting people where they were, addressing the unique needs of each person and presenting the gospel in a relevant and meaningful way. Christians involved in reaching their webs are better able to understand each person's individual needs and the appropriate ways to introduce the need-meeting alternative of Jesus Christ and His Church.

Principle No. 8—*Disciple-making is most effective when biblical insights and church growth research are integrated.*

Churches participating in *The Master's Plan for Making Disciples* are using a process built on solid biblical and theological concepts, as well as the insights of years of church growth research.

Church growth principles can make disciple-making more effective in many ways. Did you know, for example, that church growth research has found that people in your web will vary, over time, as to their "receptivity" to the gospel? Did you know it is possible to tell when they are most receptive to becoming new disciples? Or, did you know that the way a church member views the "process" of verbally sharing the gospel has an important effect on whether the non-Christian responds? Did you know that the events in the first few months of a new Christian's life often determine whether that person will continue as an active member or will lose interest and drop out?

There are many important new insights into how people come to Christ and the church that creatively and consistently support the examples of Jesus and the early Christians and provide us with a practical *process.*

Principle No. 9—*Disciple-making is most effective as a natural and continuing process.*

Continuous disciple-making requires prudent stewardship of church members' time and energy. It requires an evangelistic process that renews rather than exhausts laity. It requires a process that is a natural part of life.

When does disciple-making become a natural part of the Christian life?

1. *When it builds on natural human relationships.*
2. *When it builds on the need to love and be loved.*
3. *When it becomes part of the entire church organizational structure.*
4. *When it is self-perpetuating.*

The Master's Plan is a strategy for making disciples that has the potential for positively affecting every group and organization in the church.

5

Seven Steps for Making Disciples

Pastor Austin and Chuck had just finished a lunch together. As they returned to the church, Pastor Austin asked, "Chuck, are you witnessing to anyone at the present time?"

Chuck was not proud of his answer. "No, not really."

There was a pause in the conversation as the two entered the pastor's study and sat down. "Is that because the

"But you are witnessing to them, Chuck, even if it's not intentional."

people you relate to—your neighbors, your relatives, friends, people you work with—are already believers?"

"Oh, no," answered Chuck. "I don't think any of the people I work with are believers. Neither are my neighbors. And relatives, well, I'd say maybe half are Christians."

"And with how many of these unreached people do you have a fairly close relationship?" asked Pastor Austin.

"Well, I guess I'm on a first-name basis or better with about 9 or 10."

"So how are they responding to your witness?" asked the pastor.

At first Chuck thought he had heard wrong. "Responding? Didn't you hear what I said? I'm not witnessing to anyone."

Pastor Austin's words were disturbing. "Oh, but you are. Even if it's not intentional."

"You mean the way I act? The things I say? The things I do? That's all part of my witness?"

Pastor Austin nodded.

* * * * * * * * * *

Every day each of us comes in contact with unreached persons with whom we have ongoing, established relationships. These persons are called our "extended family."

Extended Families

If you are a father or mother, you no doubt feel an important sense of responsibility for your family. God has given you oversight for their physical health, safety, personal growth, and spiritual development.

But did you realize God has given you an extended family for whom you also have a responsibility? They are members of your *oikos*—your close friends, your relatives, and associates—who do not know Jesus Christ. In many cases you may be the only "bridge" God has to them.

EXTENDED FAMILY: A church member's close friends, relatives, and associates who are not presently in Christ and the church.

To develop your vocabulary in *The Master's Plan,* it is helpful to understand the difference between two terms: *oikos* and *extended family.*

Your *oikos* is composed of the people in your circle of influence—both Christians and non-Christians.

Your extended family, on the other hand, are the persons in your *oikos* who are not presently in Christ and the church.

* * * * * * * * * *

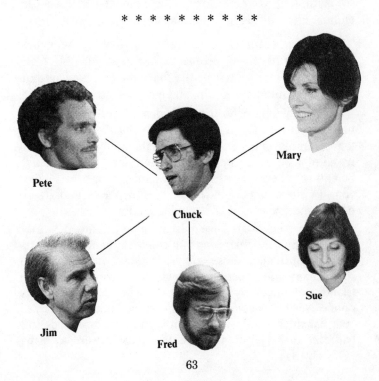

Chuck Bradley considered his own extended family; those people he knew who were not presently Christians. There was Jim, the art director at Chuck's office; Chuck's younger sister, Mary; Pete, Chuck's next door neighbor; Fred, a friend at the gym where Chuck works out twice a week; and Chuck's cousin, Sue, who lives a few miles away. Chuck saw each of these people frequently and enjoyed a mutually respected relationship with them. Yet none were Christians.

* * * * * * * * * *

So, how do you begin such a significant adventure as seeing those in your extended family come to Christ and the church? Here are seven important steps:

1. *Identify Your Extended Family.* Analyze the regular contacts you have with people in your day-to-day life. Consider the people in each of the following groups: common kinship, common friendship, and common associates.

Those people who are related biologically or through marriage constitute the *common kinship* area of your extended family. One person's immediate family may be composed of a spouse and children. For another, it may include parents, brothers, or sisters. Other family members, such as cousins, aunts, uncles, in-laws, nieces, nephews, and grandparents may be part of an extended family.

Close friends are also part of your extended family. Through *common friendship* you can identify people you regard as confidants; those you trust; those with whom you share plans and experiences, joys and sorrows. These are friends you regularly communicate with in person or by phone. Neighbors you know on a first-name basis are part of your extended family. Those you invite over for a backyard barbecue or social event, those you look forward to being with, are all part of the *common friendship* segment of your extended family.

The *common associates* area of your extended family may include people at work (or school) with whom you rub shoulders daily. Perhaps you enjoy coffee or lunch together. You share family news, talk over current events, and discuss matters of mutual interest pertaining to your work. Also in the *common associates* part of your extended family may be people with whom you do civic work or are involved with in special clubs or projects. Perhaps you solicit funds together, or work on a committee, or share a mutual concern for your city and its quality of life.

Identifying and listing those 6, 8, or 10 people who comprise your extended family is an important first step in seeing them saved and in the church.

2. *Develop a Personal Profile of Each Extended Family Member.* Franklin D. Roosevelt made it a point to become a personal friend to every dignitary he met. Before the foreign leader came to visit, the president would study the person's hobbies, special interests, and areas of personal concern. When the diplomat and the president met, they first talked on an official, political level. But then the conversation often changed. The president would praise the diplomat for any special achievements he had made, direct the discussion to the diplomat's own hobbies or interests, and listen attentively as the person spoke. Through expressions of genuine interest, Roosevelt built friendships that endured a lifetime.

Knowing a person on a level beyond biographical details of age, marital status, and occupation is part of effective disciple-making. The more we can understand the interests, concerns, and needs of our extended family members, the deeper and more substantial our relationship with them will be.

What do you know about the members of your extended

family? What is each one's personal background? What do they do in their spare time? What are their attitudes toward various subjects? How is their family life, and what concerns do they have in that area? Are they happy in their jobs? What important events are they experiencing in their lives?

What do you know about the spiritual dimension in the lives of members in your extended family? What is their previous religious experience? What knowledge do they have about the Bible? What do they understand about the Christian life? Are they open or antagonistic to discussing spiritual matters? Do they have any Christian friends?

Also, note why you think each is not a believer. Has he heard the gospel or been invited to accept Christ?

You may not know the answer to all these questions. If not, this is an important place to begin the disciple-making process—simply getting to know the person in a more meaningful way.

3. *Focus Your Efforts.* As you review the list of names in your extended family, you may want to identify several people with whom you have a natural, warm relationship. You enjoy doing things together and have a variety of common interests. They may be people who would enjoy being with your church friends. These people should be potentially receptive to the gospel and easily accepted in your congregation.

The number of people you can focus on may differ. A busy executive, for example, may have time to work effectively with only one or two people at a time, whereas a retired person could easily focus on six or more non-Christians in his extended family.

* * * * * * * * * *

Chuck Bradley identified three members of his extended family to focus on: Pete, his next door neighbor, his sister Mary, and Fred, his friend from the gym.

His neighbor, Pete, had often invited Chuck to go fishing, but so far Chuck had never gone.

Pete is married but has no children. His wife is six months pregnant. Pete's favorite recreational pastime is fishing. He repeatedly invites Chuck, but so far Chuck has never gone with him. Pete's church background is "zero."

Mary, Chuck's sister, is getting a divorce after seven years of marriage. They have no children, and she is 28 years old. Mary was once active in church, but after her marriage to a non-Christian, she became inactive. She is currently unemployed and has a high school education. She worked a few years before marriage but has acquired no marketable skills.

As for Fred, Chuck sees him twice a week at the gym where they both work out. They enjoy sharing information about their families, jobs, and the weather, but never see each other outside the gym.

* * * * * * * * * *

4. *Develop a Disciple-making Plan.* Scripture's admonition to plan carefully is particularly applicable to making disciples: "Any enterprise is built by wise planning, becomes strong through common sense, and profits wonderfully by keeping abreast of the facts" (Prov. 24:3-4, TLB). Introducing non-Christian friends and relatives to Christ, and directing their attention to the opportunity of new life, demands our best efforts. Yet often we tend to run ahead in our evangelistic methods without first considering insights that might increase our effectiveness.

Our disciple-making plans need to begin with meeting people at their point of need. Paul said, "I have become all things to all men so that by all possible means I might save some" (1 Cor. 9:22). We need to recognize the unique ways hearers perceive and personally relate the Good News to their lives and needs.

Christ introduced people to the Kingdom through events they could readily identify with. He respected them as individuals with unique interests and needs. He asked the woman at the well for a drink of water. He told stories about sowing and harvesting to people who understood such things.

Because the disciple-making plan you develop for your extended family members is so important, Chapter 7 will be entirely devoted to practical suggestions for developing an effective plan for each non-Christian in your *oikos.*

5. *Work the Disciple-making Plan.* As you implement the steps of your disciple-making plan (step 4), be sensitive to and aware of the events in your extended family member's life. There could be a right time and a wrong time, a right way and a wrong way to communicate Christ's love.

Here are some suggestions for developing effective communication skills:

A. *Attentive Listening.* A prominent theologian once said, "The first duty of love is to listen."[1] Almost everyone is born with the capacity to hear. However, the ability to listen must be deliberately learned and cultivated. Listening is a valuable skill for every layperson concerned with effective disciple-making.

Chuck had been really trying to listen to his friend Fred's ideas and opinions. He found listening to be hard work since he enjoyed talking, even to the point of monopolizing many conversations. But as he and Fred worked out in the gym, Chuck began to listen. Their friendship deepened as Fred shared more of himself with Chuck.

B. *Relating to Needs.* God's love is the greatest need-meeting resource on earth. Be alert to the unique areas of need in your extended family members.

A close and meaningful relationship includes mutual sharing of experiences—happiness, sadness, success, failure, irritation, disappointment. Around these, the importance of faith and fellowship in the church often becomes apparent. Points of need in your own life, or in the lives of your extended family members, provide opportunity to relate your experiences to theirs and to discuss the solution Christ has provided. "I will tell of the kindnesses of the Lord, the deeds for which he is to be praised, according to all the Lord has done for us" (Isa. 63:7).

Following their workout, Chuck and Fred talked in the gym dressing room. The conversation turned toward their families and Fred talked about his daughter. "Tina's mixed up with kids that Joan and I think are headed for trouble, and she just won't listen to us. Frankly, we don't know what to do, or where to turn."

"That can be pretty tough," said Chuck sympathetically. "Peer pressure can really be powerful. We had similar problems with Karen."

"What did you do about it?" asked Fred.

"Well, we've tried to let Karen know that we love her

and that God loves her." Chuck continued, "I also think that becoming more involved in the youth group at our church has been a big help."

Chuck went on to briefly describe the family counseling that his pastor provided.

Across the next several weeks Chuck was successful in getting Fred and his family to attend church with him. Fred's daughter liked the youth group and became active in it. Soon the entire family was involved. it was a special moment for Chuck when at the close of Pastor Austin's message one Sunday morning Fred and his wife came to the altar and were beautifully converted. Chuck realized then how important it had been for him to identify with Fred at his point of need.

C. *Identifying Receptive Periods.* God's love and caring is especially appropriate during significant changes in lifestyle (such as marriage, birth of a child, new job, retirement, etc.), or incidents of stress in our extended family members' lives (death of a spouse, divorce, family crisis, injury, etc.). These times are called "periods of transition." A period of transition is a span of time in which a person's or family's normal, everyday behavior patterns are disrupted by some event that puts them into an unfamiliar situation. The more recent the "transition-producing event" in the person's life, the more receptive he will be to Christ and the church.[2] It is important for your extended family members to hear the gospel at these times. A sermon, followed by a public invitation, or a personal evangelism team visiting the home, may provide the setting in which a life is committed to Christ.

D. *Appropriate Timing.* A fourth important point in responding to your extended family member is timing. *When* you communicate God's love and the Christian experience can be as important as *what* you communicate. For example, in the gym when Fred explained to Chuck his difficulty with his daughter, it was an appropriate moment for Chuck to relate how Christ guided him in similar circumstances and how the church supported them.

E. *Understandable Language.* Sharing the realities and benefits of Christ in everyday language, in the context of everyday experience, gives important credibility and relevance to the Christian faith. As you mention your faith to an extended family member, and the difference in your life because of it, speak in words and phrases the person will understand. Paul told the Christians at Colossae: "Be wise in the way you act toward outsiders; make the most of every opportunity. Let your conversation be always full of grace, seasoned with salt, so that you may know how to answer everyone" (Col. 4:5-6).

Each of the areas mentioned above will help you understand and respond more effectively to the unique concerns of your extended family member.

6. *Pray Regularly and Specifically for Each Extended Family Member.* "The prayer of a righteous man is powerful and effective" (James 5:16).

Prayer must be at the very heart of the disciple-making process. The importance of regular prayer for specific members of your extended family cannot be overemphasized.

As part of your daily prayers identify each person in your extended family by name, and pray for specific needs. Ask God for the opportunity to let His love for them be experienced through you.

Care for them. The definition of *caring* being, "Allowing God's love to flow through you to people, especially those in your network of relationships."

It may well be that the person in our extended family has never before been held up to God in prayer. What a thrill to be the first one to have the privilege! And it is impossible to talk daily with the Lord about a person and not become genuinely concerned about him and aware of caring/sharing opportunities.

Jesus promised: "If two of you on earth agree about anything you ask for, it will be done for you by my Father in heaven" (Matt. 18:19). Each layperson involved in making disciples should pray not only for the non-Christians in his own web but also for specific people in other members' extended families. Sharing prayer concerns, asking God for a sense of awareness to opportunities, and thanking Him for answered prayer are important parts of each person's role in making disciples.

7. *Accept Your Accountability to Others and to God.* A final major step in the disciple-making process is to meet regularly with other Christians similarly involved. As you discuss goals and individual experiences in regular meetings, you will find an important sense of support, fellowship, and accountability.

No member's caring relationships with extended family members will be identical with another's. Thus, sharing individual successes and failures can provide rich learning experiences. One person's insights sharpen another's understanding. And the probability of continuing as active disciple-makers is increased when members are part of such a regular group. A Sunday School class, ladies' fellowship, or men's prayer breakfast could function well here.

In these meetings, members share prayer concerns for each person in their extended families. These concerns become the subject of intercessory prayer for the entire group. Likewise, experiences of answered prayer are shared with the group and expressed in praise and thanks to the Lord.

Church members may want to become prayer partners with one another, each agreeing to pray for his partner and the people in his extended family. The disciple-making process is strengthened immeasurably as extended family members are daily and individually prayed for.

Of course, it is vitally important to invite your extended family members to church. Most witnessing efforts that culminate in a decision to accept Jesus Christ as Savior and Lord do so in the church.

Your Opportunity . . .

Is it possible to see the lives of friends, relatives, and associates really change as they encounter the miraculous love of Christ? Can you, as an "ordinary layman," have a meaningful and purposeful role in reaching these people with Christ's love? The answer is a resounding, affirmative *yes*. You can do it! In fact, you are probably *the best* person to show these extended family members His life-transforming power.

6

Planning for Conversion in the Disciple-making Process

"Amen." The words escaped Chuck's lips in joyful response to the evangelist's concluding remarks. The powerful revival message on conversion reminded Chuck of his own new birth. It had been the most important moment of his life.

As the evangelist began the invitation, Chuck silently prayed that many people would come to the altar. He thought especially of Jim, his art director at the office, for whom he and Diane had been praying. He had invited Jim to the revival but wasn't sure if he was here this Sunday morning. As he was praying Diane nudged him, "It's Jim and Pam; let's go pray with them."

Chuck and Diane moved out into the aisle behind Jim and Pam and knelt opposite them at the altar. In just a few moments Jim looked up smiling, obviously a new creature in Christ Jesus. A few moments later his wife, Pam, testified that Christ had come into her life and that she, too, had experienced the new birth.

* * * * * * * * * *

The Importance of Conversion

Conversion is the most dramatic aspect of disciple-making. While it is only one part of the total process, it is an absolutely essential step. The emphasis on disciple-making makes much of the fact that decision is not enough. Our goal is to nurture new believers to discipleship. The kind of evangelism we emphasize in the Church of the Nazarene does not end with conversion. It begins there. The Great Commission that Jesus gave His disciples does not conclude with baptism but goes on to instruction and obedience to all the things Jesus taught. "Observing" all the teachings of Jesus means that disciple-making is really producing responsible church members. Jesus founded and blessed the Church. It is clear beyond dispute that building the Church was the work of God. Christ was present in His Church in the Person of the Holy Spirit, giving it dynamic and dramatic growth.

To emphasize the process of disciple-making is not to minimize the necessity of a crisis experience. Without conversion the disciple-making process comes to a complete stop. It cannot continue. The conversion experience is the glorious step that begins the new life in Christ.

The Many Aspects of Conversion

There are a number of facets to the conversion experience. Sometimes they are viewed as steps but some of them occur simultaneously. Conversion usually follows (1) an *awareness of need* and/or (2) a *conviction of sin.* When an individual hears the gospel preached, he begins to realize he has transgressed God's law and stands in need of God's forgiveness.

Genuine conviction is usually more than a mental realization that an individual has sinned. It involves the work of the Holy Spirit impressing the heart with a sense of guilt. For some individuals the sense of guilt is not as great as the realization of need. As Saint Paul said, "God's kindness leads you toward repentance" (Rom. 2:4). Conviction is the work of the Holy Spirit in an individual's life. Response to that conviction should be (3) *repentance.*

Repentance involves not only the confession of sin but

also the abandonment of it. A person who repents does an about-face in his life. He changes direction. As Saint Paul said, "If anyone is in Christ, he is a new creation; the old has gone, the new has come!" (2 Cor. 5:17). Genuine repentance is godly sorrow for sins and a determination to turn from sinful practices.

For repentance to be productive it must be supported by (4) *faith*. Repentance without faith leads to depression, but with faith it produces the miracle of conversion. Faith is believing God will forgive the sins that have been committed. Faith is trusting Christ and believing Him for salvation. Faith is relying upon Christ totally and completely. When faith is exercised, the conversion experience is consummated. In that moment the life is (5) *regenerated*.

Regeneration is the transformational aspect of conversion. In this experience the old passes away and the new comes. At the same moment the old life is forgiven, there is a "washing of regeneration," an initial cleansing that washes away the guilt and stain of sinful practices. A person is indeed a new creature in Christ Jesus.

In this moment the person is also (6) *justified*. The legal requirements of the law are satisfied. The guilty sinner is set free from the penalty of sins. As someone has said, justification is just-as-if-I had never sinned.

Simultaneous with justification is (7) *adoption*. It is a glorious reality that when we are converted we are adopted into the family of God. John exclaims, "How great is the love the Father has lavished on us, that we should be called children of God!" (1 John 3:1). And Saint Paul says, "Now if we are children, then we are heirs—heirs of God and co-heirs with Christ" (Rom. 8:17).

The final facet of conversion is (8) *assurance*. The Spirit bears witness to the individual that he is indeed a child of God. The conversion experience does not depend upon hope. It is not based upon a vain wish. There is an up-to-date reality in the life of each believer, an assurance that he is truly a child of God. God's Spirit "testifies with our spirit" (see Rom. 8:16) and our hearts are at rest. Our hearts are assured.

The multifaceted miracle of conversion took place in the lives of Jim and Pam at the altar that morning. In those few moments a glorious transformation experience occurred in their lives. They would never be the same. Like Chuck, years later they would look back to the moment when they were first forgiven—when they became new creatures in Christ Jesus. More than any other part of the disciple-making process, this would be their hinge point. They probably would not testify to the steps leading up to their conversion or to their follow-up experiences, but again and again they would joyously testify to the glorious moment when God for Christ's sake forgave their sins and they were born again.

Approaches to Preparation

As comprehensive and powerful as the conversion experience is, it does not normally occur without preparation. Churches that are effective in evangelism and disciple-making give serious attention to the preparation that leads to conversion. Some organizations call it preevangelism, but this implies that only the conversion experience itself is evangelism. Jesus' commission was not just to tell the Good News without any concern as to whether or not people responded. Most Christians realize that response to the Good News is just as important as proclaiming it. This is why the Church of the Nazarene is committed to "persuasion evangelism" rather than just "proclamation evangelism." But whether it is called preevangelism, preparation for conversion, or the early steps of a decision-making process, the fact is that preparation for conversion is very important. A great deal of insight to this fact has been provided by James F. Engel in what has become known as "The Engel Scale." It graphically portrays the decision-making process through a series of eight steps.

THE ENGEL SCALE
The Complete Spiritual Decision Process Model

MAN'S RESPONSE

−8	Awareness of Supreme Being
−7	Some Knowledge of Gospel
−6	Knowledge of Fundamentals of Gospel
−5	Grasp of Personal Implications of Gospel
−4	Positive Attitude Toward Act of Becoming a Christian
−3	Problem Recognition and Intention to Act
−2	Decision to Act
−1	Repentance and Faith in Christ

NEW CREATURE

+1	Post Decision Evaluation
+2	Assimilation into Church
+3	Conceptual and Behavioral Growth
	• Communion with God
	• Stewardship
	• Internal Reproduction
	• External Reproduction

What the preparation, leading up to conversion, makes abundantly clear is that intentionality needs to be introduced into our plans. The Church of the Nazarene has long practiced special and concerted prayer in preparing for evangelistic activities. But even greater intentionality needs to be introduced into the program. Incorporation that was discussed in Chapter 3 is probably the most critical aspect of preparation, with the possible exception of prayer. The intentionality involved in the incorporation process has already been discussed.

Planning for conversion should include programs and

78

events in the life of the church in which people are specifically confronted with the claims of the gospel and called to decision for conversion. Three methods are commonly practiced in the Church of the Nazarene.

1. *Revivals.* Revival services are most typical of the ways people are called to conversion in the Church of the Nazarene. Nazarene revivals are probably most accurately characterized as evangelistic revivals. In most instances the goal embraces the renewal of Christians as well as the conversion of sinners. There have been claims that the traditional revival is not the effective means of calling people to conversion that it used to be. This evaluation is superficial. In reality, thousands of revivals in churches of all sizes, year after year, consistently call sinners to believe on the Lord Jesus Christ and be saved. The sheer mass of this effort exceeds the combined efforts of all other attempts at conversion.

There are several reasons why evangelistic revivals are effective. First of all, a specific time is set aside. The church recognizes it on its calendar and people generally prioritize it in their schedules. Second, everyone recognizes that a strong emphasis will be placed on calling sinners to repentance. It becomes one of the goals of the event. In the third place, significant preparation is usually put forth for a revival campaign. When it is not, the church does not maximize revival potential. Research consistently reveals that adequately prepared revivals achieve unusual results. A fourth value of revival is that a professional, or at least a person with particular competency, is called as evangelist. The evangelist normally has gifts or special abilities to confront people with the gospel or with the claims of Christ and to call them to decision and conversion. Still another value of the evangelistic revival is that corporate activity gives particular meaning to a public decision as it focuses on a time and place, and has witnesses. Indeed, the act of coming forward in a public setting is an open declaration reinforcing the conversion experience. Furthermore, it gives opportunity for the entire church to celebrate this victory in the life of the individual. The importance of revivals as a means of calling people to decision and producing conversions cannot be overemphasized in the Church of the Nazarene. It is by far the most traditional methodology for bringing people to Jesus Christ as Lord and Savior. Churches of all sizes and in every imaginable geographic location should include regular evangelistic revivals in their disciple-making plans.

2. *Personal Evangelism.* A second methodology for producing conversion is personal evangelism. This method is on the increase in the Church of the Nazarene. Efforts to reinforce this methodology go back more than a quarter of a century. The midcentury "Crusade for Souls" was a concerted denomination-wide effort to teach personal evangelism methods to Nazarenes. The advent of "Evangelism Explosion" in the '70s, and the subsequent training program developed by the Department of Evangelism, has brought widespread use of personal evangelism techniques to the Church of the Nazarene. Increasing numbers of people are being brought to Jesus Christ through personal evangelism.

Most Christians feel a sense of responsibility to tell the Good News to those who do not know Jesus Christ as Lord and Savior; yet most Christians experience feelings of guilt about their failure to do this on a regular basis. They indicate that their failure stems from their inability to articulate their faith or to help people understand what it means to become a Christian. Specific personal evangelism methodologies have been developed to enable a Christian to "give an answer to everyone who asks you to give the reason for the hope that you have" (1 Pet. 3:15).

There are several popular methods, including the "Four Spiritual Laws" or the Nazarene adaption, "Life Can Have

True Meaning." But the techniques of "Evangelism Explosion" have been more widely taught and used throughout the Church of the Nazarene than any other methodology. Such training is promoted by Evangelism Ministries and is available from regional evangelism coordinators.

The strength of personal evangelism is that it provides a person-to-person discussion enabling the prospect to discuss items in the presentation of the gospel that he may not understand. The encounter normally takes place in the individual's home, which overcomes some of the timidity factors that exist in a public service. It precludes the opportunity to hide in the crowd to avoid being confronted with the gospel. The personal evangelism encounter also makes it possible to lead the person through the major factors, which need to be considered in order to come to the point of accepting Jesus Christ as Lord and Savior.

Generally when persons experience conversion in their homes, they want to declare this publicly in one of the regular services. Most churches give them opportunity to come forward at the close of the Sunday morning or Sunday evening service. While personal evangelism should not be viewed as a replacement for public evangelism, it should definitely be included as an important supplement. A church that is serious about evangelism will hold annual training sessions in personal evangelism techniques.

3. *Regular Services.* The third method of calling people to conversion is the regular service. This has been an effective means of producing conversion throughout the history of the Church of the Nazarene. While it resembles the evangelistic revival service, it is far more pervasive. Revivals normally occur two or three times a year, while most churches have at least one invitation a month. Many will open the altar after every sermon. The average is probably two or three altar invitations per month.

There is, of course, a normalness in regular services that removes for visitors and prospects the fear of being confronted with the claims of the gospel. Consistent proclamation of the gospel makes its impact upon them and when they are ready to respond, the opportunity is ever present.

It is vitally important that pastors plan regular times when they call people to conversion and give them an opportunity to respond. The necessity of being specific in this regard cannot be overemphasized. General appeals have their place but there must be regular times when the pastor preaches for decision and calls people to immediate response.

New Convert Follow-Through

Just as it is important to prepare for conversion and plan for calling people to decision, it is also important to understand that conversion does not complete the disciple-making process. There are many steps that need to follow conversion.

Most churches are unaware of the spiritual nurture new converts need during the first few hours, days, and weeks of their new life in Christ. Churches talk about follow-through, but they generally mean something other than spiritual nurture. They are usually thinking more in terms of maturity and training for service. What is needed most is to help the new converts understand what has happened in their lives. They will question, "What is the meaning of this experience? Was it a good thing or not? If it was, where do I go from here?"

Christians need to regard the new convert much like a baby, for he is totally helpless spiritually and must be fed and cared for. Satan will certainly tempt him to doubt the reality of his conversion experience. Reassurance of faith from God's Word is vital. Though this is best taught one-on-one, new Christians must also learn how to draw nourishment on their own through God's Word and prayer with good devotional practices. Mature Christians can help new converts learn to meet and overcome temptations that are sure to come.

This spiritual nurture phase is probably the most important aspect of follow-through. In-depth Bible studies to help the new Christian understand God's Word more comprehensively, and involvement in Sunday School and other Christian education activities are also important.

The convert should be encouraged early in his new life to take membership instruction and join the church. The Christian education process should include understanding spiritual gifts so new converts can perceive how the Body of Christ functions. It should also include training them to serve the Lord in specific and effective ways so they can work out their faith in service to God, the church, and their fellowman.

Entire Sanctification

In the Church of the Nazarene we believe the disciple-making process does not end with church membership and involvement. A second crisis in the disciple-making process is entire sanctification. At some point in the life of every Christian comes the realization that something is lacking in his ability to maintain spiritual victory, and the Word of God holds up a model that does not correspond with his Christian experience. He needs to learn that obedience to Christ and His Word is crucial and through consecration and commitment of his life and the surrender of his will, the Holy Spirit cleanses of inbred sin and endows him with power for life and service. This experience is wrought in the heart of the believer by faith and is witnessed to by the Holy Spirit.

Both the crisis of conversion and the second crisis of entire sanctification are essential steps in the disciple-making process. Crises should be goals and checkpoints, yet not ends in themselves. Churches should not allow themselves to think they can abandon the person who has been converted and sanctified wholly. We cannot expect these people to come to maturity on their own. This is not the Master's plan for making disciples.

7

Reaching Your "Extended Family"

It was late afternoon and Diane Bradley invited her friend Judy for a quick cup of coffee. This had become a regular ritual since Judy returned to work. Judy was recently divorced and is the mother of three small children. She's working again, not because she wants to but because she has to.

"Diane, it's so frustrating to work as a clerk typist in the same office I once managed," said Judy.

"Diane, it's so frustrating to work as a clerk-typist in the same office I once managed."

"Judy, that must be hard," replied Diane sympathetically.

"And all because I took 10 years out to start a family." Judy brought her cup to the kitchen sink. "Well, enough of this crying on your shoulder. I've got to get home and relieve the sitter. Thanks for the coffee."

"You're welcome, Judy. Maybe next week we could get together for lunch."

"I'd like that."

After Judy left, Diane breathed a silent prayer for her divorced friend. She asked particularly for wisdom in knowing the best ways to show Judy that God loved her.

* * * * * * * * * *

Strategy for Reaching Friends and Relatives

One of the most important steps in reaching friends and relatives in your extended family will be developing an appropriate and effective strategy for introducing those people to Christ and His Body.

1. *Caring.* Your most important role as a witness to them is personifying Christ's love. *God's love is best seen and experienced by others through our love.*

Consider the *burden-lifting* implications of this concept. The traditional requirements of a "good" witness (verbal fluency, extrovertive personality, tenacity) become less important than simply being an open channel through which God's love can be expressed and experienced by those in your extended family. Think of it: You become the channel for God's love! Exciting? Yes! Possible? Absolutely!

"For I was hungry and you gave me something to eat, I was thirsty and you gave me something to drink, I was a stranger and you invited me in, I needed clothes and you clothed me, I was sick and you looked after me, I was in prison and you came to visit me" (Matt. 25:35-36).

The people in your extended family may not require clothing, food, or water. But they do have real needs. Responding to the void of loneliness, frustration, or despair demands a personal investment of genuine caring.

Christ is a model for our caring relationships with extended family members. The caring aspect of making disciples reflects God's very nature: "God is love."

Our caring and friendship with others must be *unconditional.* It is not the bait of a religious trap. Nor is it the scheming means to an ultimate end. Unconditional caring reflects God's unswerving, unrelenting love. If a friend were to say, "I don't want anything to do with your religion," should your caring be any less than before? Do you think God's love is any less for those who reject Him? If anything, God's concern is even greater. How many people have once rejected His love and later, perhaps in a time of need, responded and are now active, reproducing Christians? Caring must be genuine and unconditional, not dependent on how the person responds to spiritual overtures.

2. *Strengthening Relationships.* Your disciple-making effectiveness is enhanced where strong relationships exist with members of your extended family. The apostle John writes, "Dear friends, let us love one another, for love comes from God. Everyone who loves has been born of God and knows God" (1 John 4:7).

What person does not enjoy the companionship of a loving, caring friend! A strong, growing relationship between you and your extended family member contributes immeasurably to allowing the Holy Spirit to speak to that person.

In *The Friendship Factor* McGinnis says, "It is no accident so many important encounters occurred between Jesus and His friends when they were at the table. There is some-

Strong relationships come with shared experiences.

thing almost sacramental about breaking bread with one another."[1]

Invite your friend to a special event you both will enjoy. Drop by his home with something from your garden, workshop, or flowerbed. Or make a point to have lunch together once a week. Has your friend mentioned a special need that could be a point of relationship building, such as helping lay a brick wall, hanging drapes, or painting the house? Shared experiences build strong friendships with few words having to be spoken.

The idea of "friendship evangelism"—an approach that encourages Christians to make friends in order to win them to Christ—is not new. But it would be a mistake to interpret this emphasis to mean the manipulation of a person or scheming to get a decision. There is a significant difference between the *reason* for a relationship (to get a "convert") and the result of a caring relationship. Build your friendship with sincerity and unconditional caring.

Your greatest resource in developing a meaningful and caring friendship is in simply being yourself—natural and unmasked. The phrase "I'm not perfect, just forgiven" reflects a healthy attitude in recognizing the shortcomings each person has. The unique benefit of the Christian life is in the strength and support from a source greater than ourselves. When your extended family member understands this simple truth, it may change his entire attitude toward faith and life in Christ.

As you spend time with your extended family member, your sense of values and purpose in life naturally surface. In his book *Power in Praise,* Carothers observes that if we grumble and complain as bitterly as our non-Christian friends over the many little upsetting incidents of the day, others conclude that our faith does no more than occupy an hour of our time

As you spend time with your extended family member, your sense of values and purpose in life naturally surfaces.

Sunday morning.[2] How do you react to delays or difficulties on the job; to emergencies; to everyday encounters? Do you respond in a way that causes non-Christian friends and relatives to see a difference that suggests the quality of your life in Christ?

3. *Enhancing Your Witness.* As you think and plan how to communicate God's love to your extended family, the question naturally arises, "But what do I say?" To find the answer, let's turn to the Bible.

Jesus, in teaching His disciples to be fishers of men, used many different models. From Nicodemus, the religious ruler who was told he needed to be "born again," to the woman of Samaria who was offered the water of eternal life, to the thief on the cross who asked only to be remembered when Christ came into His kingdom. Each situation presents different needs, portrays different relationships, uses different words, brings a different response. However, while there was not one formula, there were common denominators of the gospel presentations that surfaced again and again.

The assumption—the sinfulness of people. Because we have all sinned, the gospel embodies a call to repentance and faith: Isa. 53:6; Eccles. 7:20; Rom. 3:23; 3:20; 1 John 1:8.

The focal point—Jesus Christ. People in the New Testament did not respond to a series of theological propositions. They responded to a person—Jesus Christ.

The target for witness—responsive people. Jesus instructed His disciples to identify receptive people and communicate the Good News to them: Matt. 13:9; John 4:35; Matt. 13:23.

The starting place—the person's need. The Christian commitment seen in Scripture is based on a faith that makes people whole. "He said to her, 'Daughter, your faith has healed you. Go in peace and be freed from your suffering'"

(Mark 5:34). "It is not the healthy who need a doctor, but the sick" (Matt. 9:12).

The instrument—people. God uses people in most cases to bring other people to himself. Conversions do not take place in a vacuum. Philip interpreted the Scripture for the Ethiopian. Peter helped Cornelius. Paul helped Lydia.

The proclamation—essentials. There were important essentials that comprised the first Good News preached by all the apostles. At Pentecost Peter preached, "God has made this Jesus, whom you crucified, both Lord and Christ. . . . Repent and be baptized . . . that your sins may be forgiven" (Acts 2:36, 38). Paul proclaimed that Christ, ". . . appeared in a body, was vindicated by the Spirit, was seen by angels, was preached among the nations, was believed on in the world, was taken up in glory" (1 Tim. 3:16). In First Corinthians Paul summarizes the gospel, then says, "Whether, then, it was I or they, this is what we preach, and this is what you believed" (1 Cor. 15:11).

The goal—repentance/conversion. The basic elements of the message were proclaimed with the goal of persuading the hearers to a repentance and faith that produced new life in Christ. John the Baptist, Jesus, Peter, Paul . . . all called for repentance: Matt. 3:2; Mark 1:15; Acts 2:38; 8:22; 17:30; 26:20.

Sharing Your Faith: Four Suggestions

Here are some specific suggestions to help you share your faith verbally with others, especially those in your extended family. They are built on the biblical example and models.

1. *Know the Gospel.* Develop a clear understanding of the basics of your faith—man's sin; Christ's incarnation, death, and resurrection; repentance; salvation; etc. The more appropriate scriptures you know, the more comfortable you will feel. While proclaiming the gospel is more than simply reciting Bible verses, having a grasp of scriptures concerning

Christ's love and how one enters into the kingdom of God is an important part of the process.

2. *Be Able to Verbalize the Reasons for the Hope That Is Within You* (see 1 Pet. 3:15). You should be able to testify clearly to your own conversion to Christ. Describe the events that brought you to repentance, faith, and into the church. Be confident in expressing "why" and "how" Jesus is Lord in your life. Some people find it helpful to write out their testimony and memorize it. Others rehearse it with a friend. Whatever means you use, be able to share your personal experience clearly, concisely, and in words understandable to a non-Christian.

3. *Be Sensitive to the Spiritual Needs and Receptivity of Those in Your Extended Family.* Skills of listening, of empathy, of identification, of relating the gospel and the church to relevant needs will be of great value in knowing when and how to share the Good News. Asking questions will help you determine where your friends are in their spiritual journey.

4. *Be Open to the Holy Spirit's Direction.* In most cases the Holy Spirit uses people to bring other people to Christ. Isn't it exciting that He has chosen you to be a witness of His eternal grace? Isn't it affirming that He believes in you enough to open doors where you can communicate saving faith? When you say, "Here I am, Lord, send me" it opens a door that leads into enlarged ministry, usefulness, blessing, and joy.

Provide for a Variety of Exposures

Each church member should be able to express comfortably the meaning of Christ in his life to a non-Christian friend. A dialogue between two friends on the subject of the church and Christianity would include sharing one's personal experience. There is an important credibility in such sharing between two respected friends.

As you plan ways to communicate God's love to members of your extended family, realize that there are additional ways to communicate the message—perhaps more persuasively. The pastor, a special evangelistic film, a guest teacher or speaker, a revival campaign, or a church member with the gift of evangelism may be able to present the gospel in a more compelling way than you. Actually, most people who end up as active Christians and responsible church members have heard the gospel more than once from more than one source, prior to making their decision for Christ. One particular research study found that those who were vital Christians and active church members had heard the gospel presented six different times before they made their Christian commitment.[3] This fairly high number of exposures to the gospel among the group of active Christians was in sharp contrast to the number of times the gospel was heard among people who made a decision but soon became inactive. On the average, church dropouts heard the gospel only twice prior to their decision.

This leads to some important insights about communicating the Good News to your extended family members. People who come to Christ and become active members of your church need to have several exposures to the gospel (and the *implications* of their life-changing decision).

This need for a variety of evangelistic exposures means a church needs to provide adequate opportunities for members to bring their non-Christian friends and relatives. Worship services, revival meetings, Sunday School classes, special services, etc., may be one means in this process. Another means some churches use is to provide personal evangelism training. In these classes, laypersons discover how to give their testimonies and present the gospel using scriptures and illustrations that lead the prospect to trust Christ alone for salvation.

Other events and material may also be needed to provide support to the church member. Films, printed material, special outings and social events, home Bible studies, special interest seminars can be used as ways to provide exposure to the Good News. The key insight is not only *what* the particular means of communication is but also the *number* and *variety* of exposures—how many times and from how many sources has your extended family member been exposed to a portion of the Good News through the church? The more exposure he has, the better the chances of his understanding the love of Christ and becoming a responsible church member. Look for ways to help bring this about.

It is vitally important that the variety of exposures include occasions when people are called to conversion. While the goal is disciples rather than decisions that are not followed by discipleship, we must recognize that decision is an essential aspect of discipleship. Unless people are confronted with the claims of Christ and challenged to "choose this day whom you will serve" they may misunderstand the necessity of personal repentance and placing their trust in Christ to save them from their sins. This does not mean forcing people to decide prematurely but making sure the fruit is harvested when it is ripe.

* * * * * * * * * *

Chuck Bradley and his neighbor Pete were enjoying a growing friendship. Before Chuck identified Pete as a member of his extended family, the two had had only a casual "Hello, how are you?" acquaintance. Chuck knew that Pete's wife was expecting her first baby in a few months and that Pete's favorite recreation was fishing. Beyond that, they had seldom talked about anything more than the weather.

But as a result of his commitment to making disciples, Chuck made it a point to strengthen his friendship with Pete. He went fishing with him and even helped Pete paint his house. Twice he invited Pete to go on fishing trips with men from the church who shared Pete's fishing passion.

On the day Pete became a father, he dashed over to tell the news to Chuck and Diane. Later, when the two were alone, Pete spoke confidentially: "You know, Chuck, when my son was born last night, I never felt happier. But it was the strangest thing, I found myself bawling like a baby. Wasn't that crazy?"

"I don't think it was crazy at all, Pete," Chuck replied. "I remember I did the same thing when Karen was born."

"No kidding?" Pete asked.

"That's right."

"You know, being a father is kind of new to me," Pete said.

"You know, being a father is kind of new to me," Pete said. "And I've been doing a lot of thinking. I really need to clean up my act. You know having a kid, that's a heavy responsibility."

Actually, this turn of events caught Chuck without

much to say. As he thought about it later, he realized he sort of "blew it." Pete was receptive and would have listened had Chuck shared how his faith helped him as a father. But all Chuck said was, "Hey, Pete, our church has a good class for new parents. It deals with a lot of things that are really helpful. You and Marlene might really get something out of it. Plus, you'd meet other couples who are going through the same thing for the first time."

But Chuck's "missed opportunity" didn't prove to be fatal, because Pete and his wife joined the class for new parents, which was their first contact with the church.

Later, Pete and his wife attended other church-related activities, including Sunday worship. In time both came to the altar and committed their lives to Jesus Christ. As Chuck looked back, he saw that almost one year had elapsed from the time he first identified Pete as a member of his extended family.

The way Pete was saved and his subsequent assimilation into the church is an excellent example of *The Master's Plan* in action. Planting and watering must be done, and then, in the right season God gives the increase.

8

Your Church—Partner in Disciple-making

Christ has ordained that the Good News be proclaimed by His Church. The Church is absolutely essential to the disciple-making process. The Church is not *a* Body of Christ, it is *the* Body of Christ; not just *a* bride of Christ, but *the* bride of Christ. It is the central part of God's plan for making His good news known.[1]

In your plans for reaching the members of your extended family, your church can immeasurably increase your effectiveness in communicating the Good News and in helping them become active, responsible members. Actually, disciple-making in *The Master's Plan* cannot occur without the local church. The church is as important to effective disciple-making as any other single element. What do we mean?

Church-centered Disciple-making

The central role of the church in making disciples is based on an important concept in *The Master's Plan for Making Disciples.* The concept is called "church-centered disciple-making."

CHURCH-CENTERED DISCIPLE-MAKING—An intentional strategy and priority of the church that initiates disciple-making, trains members in disciple-making, plans regular opportunities for conversion, uses resources of the Body, creates support resources, and assimilates new believers into the church.

Church-centered disciple-making puts the church—as a corporate body—at the center of the evangelism process. It includes the church as a major partner in the disciple-making endeavor. Here are seven important contributions the local church makes to effective disciple-making:

1. *The Church's Ministry—Instilling a "Great Commission Conscience" in Its Members and Organizations.* A "Great Commission conscience" is the conviction among members that their church has the mandate, opportunity, and responsibility to communicate the gospel to nonbelievers. In the church with a Great Commission conscience, a disciple-making mentality permeates every facet and organization of its Body. The result is a genuine concern by each member for the salvation of friends, relatives, and neighbors outside of Christ. A Great Commission conscience is fostered and kindled by church leaders who are enthused about and devoted to making disciples, and who constantly hold up the disciple-making goal as a priority of the church's reason for being.

A Great Commission conscience is developed through preaching and Bible study focused on God's unswerving purpose to save lost mankind. It is created as members are clearly taught the biblical foundations of caring for and reaching people outside of Christ. It is taught in Sunday School classes, small-group fellowship meetings, in women's circles, in home cell groups. It is reflected in the lives of church officers, boards, committees, men's groups, women's groups, and youth groups. It is modeled in personal evangelism training classes and during revival campaigns. It is a "philosophy of ministry" that permeates the entire life of the church. A Great Commission conscience means that the entire church, and all of its parts, thinks and acts in response to the Great Commission.[2]

2. *The Church's Ministry—Equipping Its Members to Participate in the Great Commission.* Church leaders have a scriptural mandate to equip the saints for the work of ministry. "To prepare God's people for works of service, so that the body of Christ may be built up until we all reach unity in the faith and in the knowledge of the Son of God and become mature, attaining to the whole measure of the fullness of Christ" (Eph. 4:12-13).

The church's ministry—equipping its members to participate in the Great Commission.

The education ministry of your church is a natural place to help members understand the scope of their salvation, how to communicate their witness, the basic convictions of the gospel, and how to point a friend to Christ. Peter's words are crystal clear: "Always be prepared to give . . . the reason for the hope that you have" (1 Pet. 3:15).

Helping each member acknowledge and use his spiritual gift(s) is another task of the church in equipping members to fulfill the Great Commission. Each Christian does possess a spiritual gift(s) that can be used in disciple-making, and some discover they have the gift of evangelism. The church with a Great Commission conscience uses *all* the gifts of its members to communicate God's love to others.

3. *The Church's Ministry—Helping Members Develop Plans and Strategies to Reach Extended Families.* The most natural and most responsive place to begin disciple-making in your church is within each member's own web of influence. Members of Sunday School classes, home Bible study groups, sports teams, and cell groups can all begin to focus on the people in their webs and develop plans for seeing them come to Christ and the church.

Very important contributions to our disciple-making plans are the regular services and revival meetings when the gospel is preached and people are called to decision. Confronting people with the absolute necessity of making a definite commitment to Christ produces the "harvest" toward which our efforts have been exerted.

4. *The Church's Ministry—Providing Motivation, Encouragement, and Accountability for Member's Disciple-making Efforts.* Members are most effective in disciple-making when the church structures regular encouragement, guidance, and accountability into the process. An important part of this support is providing opportunities for regular meetings to report progress, share triumphs, and relate experiences. Such

church-sponsored "Support Team" groups encourage members in their commitment. As members share their disciple-making goals and concerns, they feel a sense of community.

SUPPORT TEAM—A group of church members (for example, a Sunday School class) who meet together regularly to encourage one another and learn how to more effectively communicate God's love to extended family members.

The church encourages members as it publicly and personally affirms them in their disciple-making efforts. Regular support and visibility of disciple-making successes shows that it is significant in the eyes of church leaders and basic to the goals of the congregation.

5. *The Church's Ministry—Complementing Members' Disciple-making Efforts.* As we saw earlier, when non-Christians have a variety of opportunities to hear the gospel and see it demonstrated, there is a much greater likelihood that they will be saved. The church is a unique resource where extended family members can see the Christian faith demonstrated in a variety of settings, by a variety of people. Revivals, music performances, recreation and sporting events, special-interest groups, mission presentations, church school learning experiences, can all creatively exemplify God's love and provide those varieties of exposure. Interaction between extended family members and church members is an important part of a successful disciple-making plan.

In his dissertation study, Dr. Flavil Yeakley analyzed the differences between the decision process of people who continued as active Christian disciples, and those who soon dropped out. He concluded that "when a person has no meaningful contact with the congregation in the process of his conversion, he is likely to feel no meaningful sense of identification with the congregation after his conversion and therefore he is likely to drop out."[3] Every opportunity for non-Christians to rub shoulders with church members provides an additional personification of Christ's love. Outsiders catch the warm, caring spirit. They sense the reality of Christ's presence that affects lives.

6. *The Church's Ministry—Meeting Needs of Extended Family Members.* A church effectively supporting members' disciple-making activities will plan programs and services around the needs and interests of extended family members.

How does a church discover the needs and concerns of extended family members? Often the simplest way is to ask individual members involved in the disciple-making process. Lyle Schaller says, "If you want to find out people's needs, ask them."[4] As church members identify and strengthen their relationships with the members of their extended family, they naturally become aware of the interests, concerns, life situations, moments of stress. Communication lines must be kept open between church leaders who influence programming and members who seek ways to respond to the needs of their extended family members.

7. *The Church's Ministry—Organizing and Administering the Disciple-making Process.* "Where there is no vision, the people perish" (Prov. 29:18, KJV). Churches eager to help members discover their disciple-making potential have little problem with morale and involvement as the process begins to flourish. But there are important administrative responsibilities to be carried out.

Personnel are necessary to coordinate disciple-making strategy and implement each step. Since most volunteers are already overworked, making disciples may require "clearing the decks" of competing interests.

The commitment to making disciples will be reflected in

the *church budget.* Adequate financial support of revivals and other disciple-making activities will really determine whether the church is serious about supporting its members in this effort.

Evaluation is important. Church leaders should regularly examine the church's disciple-making efforts by looking closely at their own experience, other members' experiences, and actual results. Regular evaluation will enable leaders to refine strategy so as to build on strengths and eliminate problems. Evaluation should focus on the training process in disciple-making, member involvement levels, church support activities, and assimilation effectiveness.

Your Church's "POTENTIAL CONGREGATION"

Here is a powerful concept that will help translate "church-centered disciple-making" into the natural flow of your church's plans and activities. It should soon become a way of thinking for every church leader, officer, and staff member. The concept: your "Potential Congregation."

POTENTIAL CONGREGATION—The cumulative group of your church members' extended families.

Let's take a closer look at the idea of your church's potential congregation since it has important implication to the success of every church member's plan for reaching his extended family.

Disciple-making Through Your Church's Potential Congregation

Your church records presently identify a group of individuals and families who comprise the "members of your congregation." These people are listed in the membership book and are people about whom various information may be kept. Most church leaders feel that the church is responsible for these members, should care for their needs, and provide opportunity through the church for personal and spiritual growth.

Functionally, the church is larger than its membership. It includes people who attend occasionally and who look to the church for ministry in special times. The church that gives high priority to disciple-making will add to its list the people in the extended families of its members. This group is the church's potential congregation.

In so redefining its "congregation," the church enlarges and extends its view of ministry beyond its present members to include all its potential disciples. Now your church is not only serving existing members—who might be called the "Worshiping Congregation"—but its potential congregation as well. Like your worshiping congregation, the members of your potential congregation can be identified by name, information can be gathered on each, their needs can be identified, and programs can be developed for them.

When You Identify Your Potential Congregation . . .

What is the impact of such a new view of your church and congregational responsibilities? How will it affect your church's outreach strategy and planning?

Here are six important implications:

1. *Your Church, When It Identifies Its Potential Congregation, Focuses on a Specific and Identifiable Group of Winnable People.* The members of your potential congregation are people outside the Body of Christ, *but* people inside the extended families of present members; therefore they are very closely related to your church. The people within your church's potential congregation are significantly more reach-

able and winnable than those not in the web of present members.

2. *Your Church, When It Identifies Its Potential Congregation, Focuses Its Caring Ministry.* Caring is a beautiful and important function of the Body of Christ. Too often, however, people have to be on the "inside" to experience it. In your potential congregation an exciting new possibility opens. Caring continues to be a major function in the life of the congregation, but it is focused not only on the needs and concerns of its present members, but also on the members of your potential congregation. The church that focuses its caring ministry on both present and potential members will see significant results as the potential congregation responds and new disciples are born. The church is exemplifying the love of God in His name.

3. *Your Church, When It Identifies Its Potential Congregation, Focuses Programming to Meet Needs.* Most ministries in a church are planned for the members of that congregation. The "youth ministry" is for the youth in the church. The "music ministry" is generally for the benefit and involvement of members in the church. The "minister of education" is paid to organize Christian education to nurture church members.

A potential congregation will help your church evaluate and prioritize its programming. While still focusing on needs and interests of members, the expanded definition means programs and plans now include potential congregation members as well. Of course, every event in the church is not expected to focus on both groups. But over the course of the church year, there should be equal consideration given to each group in the overall planning, development, and appropriation of church resources.

4. *Your Church, When It Identifies Its Potential Congregation, Experiences Increased Morale.* Contagious enthusiasm and excitement invariably result when members see their

longtime friends and relatives saved and growing in Christ in their church. Morale also builds as new Christians, who are invariably enthusiastic about their newfound dimension in life, become active in the church. Reaching out to members of your potential congregation and making them disciples can unharness spiritual growth and vitality in your church beyond your expectations.

5. *Your Church, When It Identifies Its Potential Congregation, More Effectively Invests Its Resources.* An obvious concern of church leaders is good stewardship of resources. Poor stewardship invests the church's time, money, and most valuable commodity—people—in areas that do not produce fruit. This does not happen when resources are invested in a church's potential congregation. They are the most receptive groups of people in your community. It is simply good stewardship to do your part to bring them into the Kingdom.

Because your church has identified these specific groups of people (members' extended families) to whom you seek to communicate God's love, you can accurately evaluate the effectiveness of various ministries in terms of new Christian disciples. Some approaches and programs for these people will be more productive than others. Strategy should be based on the ministries that bring results.

6. *Your Church, When It Idenfities Its Potential Congregation, Experiences a Continually Expanding Congregation.* As members of your potential congregation make commitments to Christ and become members of the Body and the worshiping congregation they have their own webs of influence. They can now identify members in their extended families and increase the church's potential congregation. And so the process begins again. This is exactly the way the Early Church grew . . . first by addition (Acts 2:47), then by multiplication (Acts 6:7).

* * * * * * * * * *

The various Support Team members had been taking turns hosting the meeting every other week. Chuck and Diane arrived at Bob Odman's apartment and spent a few minutes in informal fellowship before Tim, the team coordinator, convened the meeting.

One by one members shared what had been happening in their disciple-making endeavors since their previous meeting. Steve told about his cousin and how they had gone out for a hamburger one evening last week. "We didn't talk about religion or anything," Steve said. "But we're starting to get to know each other a lot better. We've shared some personal feelings and there's a good level of trust building."

"Sounds encouraging," Tim said. "Have you introduced your cousin to anyone else in the church?"

"No, I guess I should do that," Steve reflected.

After the discussion about Steve's cousin, another member of the group spoke up. "As you know, I've been working with two people in my web—my sister Helen, and my next door neighbor, Jim Herman. To tell you the truth, I'm kind of frustrated. It seems like nothing much has been happening in the last couple of months, particularly with my neighbor."

"What seems to be the problem?" asked Tim.

"Well, you see, I don't have much in common with him."

"I know what you mean," said Chuck. "When I was focusing on my neighbor Pete, all he ever talked about was fishing. I hate fishing. I almost gave up. But one time I brought Andrew along. He loves fishing. Well, he and Pete hit it off pretty well. Maybe you could introduce your neighbor to someone in the church who has more in common with him."

"He does have a thing about gardening, especially flowers. Tim, you play in the dirt, don't you?"

"Well, I enjoy gardening, if that's what you mean," said

Tim. "You know there's a horticultural show down at the center next week. Why don't I stop by and see if he wants to go? You ought to go along too, though."

"Sure, I'll go."

The meeting went on another 30 minutes, with other members sharing their disciple-making progress and talking through additional plans for communicating God's love to extended family members. Some reported real progress, while others had to be encouraged to "wait on the Lord."

Tim then led the group in a 15-minute Bible study. They were studying various personalities in the New Testament and how each had responded to the Great Commission. This particular evening they studied about the apostle Barnabas.

Following the Bible study, Tim passed out copies of a list of upcoming church-sponsored activities that might be appropriated in their disciple-making plans. The list included various sports events, social outings, and seminars designed to be part of the church's disciple-making support strategy.

The group concluded with prayer for each extended family member mentioned that night, and then set the time and place for the next Support Team meeting.

9

Assimilating New Disciples into the Church

This was the night for paying monthly household bills. Those who knew Chuck well, like his wife, Diane, and his daughter, Karen, made it a point to avoid the den that entire evening. To make matters worse, Chuck's calculator had expired with only half the bills paid.

Then the phone rang. Chuck didn't even make a pre-

Chuck, despite his state of frustration, was smiling! And what was more unusual, there were tears in his eyes.

tense about hiding his frustration. The caller was Mary, his sister.

Diane walked by the door just as the phone rang and looked in to see an amazing sight. Chuck, despite his state of frustration, was smiling! And what was more unusual, there were tears in his eyes.

A very curious Diane broke her long-standing rule and entered Chuck's den on bill-paying night to find out what was going on.

Chuck hung up the phone, turned to Diane, and continued to smile.

"Sweetheart, that was Mary, my sister. One of the personal evangelism teams from the church went to see her this evening and she recommitted her life to Christ."

Diane gave her husband a warm hug. "And to think that just a little over a year ago you were insisting you couldn't possibly be a witness!"

"Well, Diane, much as I hate to admit it, I guess I was wrong."

"Chuck, did I hear you say you were wrong? Now that is hard to believe."

Another phone call saved Chuck from having to respond. It was Pastor Austin.

"Yes, Pastor, she did call. Yes, I do understand my responsibility for both of them."

What Pastor Austin was reminding Chuck about was the vital importance of new disciples like Pete and Mary being successfully assimilated into the church.

"Unless they become responsible members of the church," the pastor had rightly said, "and assume their own place in the Body, the disciple-making process is incomplete."

* * * * * * * * *

ASSIMILATION—The process by which new Christians and church members come to understand and feel they are truly an accepted and trusted member of the fellowship.

It is true. Evangelism is not complete without the new Christian becoming an active part of the local church. There are some important things to remember about the process of assimilating a new member.

Characteristics of an Assimilated Member

Six months after his sister Mary had joined the church, Chuck was optimistic about her growing level of involvement and identification with the church. He had good reason to be, based on the way Mary conformed to the following nine characteristics of an assimilated member.

1. *An Assimilated Member Identifies with the Goals of the Church.* A clear statement of the goals and priorities the church holds as central to its purpose, will provide an important point for members—especially new members—to rally around. For many newcomers these goals are the only thing they have in common with other members. The specific goals of a church should: (1) be directed toward accomplishing the purpose for which the church exists; (2) be clearly measurable and achievable, and include events/activities that will reach those goals; (3) be communicated clearly to church members (especially new members); and (4) describe how people can become involved. The goals should be reviewed yearly. New members should be encouraged to become actively involved in and identified with one or more of these specific goals.

One of the first topics of the new members class that Mary was participating in concerned the stated philosophy and goals of the church. Pastor Austin presented the various statements of purpose and how the programs and ministries all related to those goals. He then explained the importance of each member's commitment to these directives through various opportunities for involvement.

2. *An Assimilated Member Is Regular in Worship Attendance.* Nearly everyone would agree that an active, responsible church member participates regularly in worship. For most Christians, Sunday morning is the focal point in the church calendar. It is that designated time when the people of God come together to worship Him and to strengthen the church-wide celebration of the Christian faith. A new Christian not participating in the worshiping life of the church is certainly missing a critical time of corporate and personal "feeling" and growing in the Word.

In the six months since Mary had committed her life to Christ, she had missed only one worship service. She had even taken part in several of the services, reading the scripture and reporting on the "new neighbor outreach" program she was involved in.

3. *An Assimilated Member Feels a Sense of Spiritual Growth and Progress.* It is important for every Christian to feel a sense of movement and spiritual growth. This is especially true for the new Christian who has so much to learn and know about this new life in Christ. Formal, as well as informal, Christian education should begin immediately. A special class for new Christians is always valuable in helping them understand their new faith.

Chuck could see almost daily growth in Mary's spiritual life. The Bible study group she was part of on Thursday mornings was a big part of her week. Mary was enthusiastically involved in her Sunday School class, which was studying Romans, and she was starting to tell Chuck things she had learned in her study that even Chuck didn't know.

4. *An Assimilated Member Has Taken Necessary Steps*

of Affiliation with the Body. It is important that the new Christian join the church soon after his Christian commitment, and thus officially identify with the Body. Such a step gives the new Christian a sense of beginning. It also gives the church Body formal notification that a new member is in their presence and they should be open and welcoming of that new member.

Following her recommitment to Christ and instruction by Pastor Austin on what it meant to be a Christian and member of that church, Mary joined the church. Following the service, she and 14 other new members were the guests of honor at a church fellowship. There Mary and the others each gave personal testimonies of how they had come to Christ. Eleven of the new members reflected how some person or persons in the church had played an important part in their coming to Christ and the church. it was an exciting and rewarding time for everyone involved.

5. *An Assimilated Member Has New Friends in the Church.* The number of new Christian friends a person makes during the first six months of church life directly influences whether that person continues as an active member, or drops out. The following chart, adapted from an article in *Church Growth: America* magazine,[1] compares 100 people who recently made a Christian decision, 50 who are now active in their church, and 50 who have since dropped out. The chart compares the number of friends each group made in the church during the first six months.

Number of New Friends in the Church	0	1	2	3	4	5	6	7	8	9+
Actives	0	0	0	1	2	2	8	13	12	12
Drop-outs	8	13	14	8	4	2	1	0	0	0

Notice the striking difference between the number of new friends the active members could identify (for example, 13 of the now active members could identify 7 new friends, 12 active members could identify 8 new friends, 12 could identify 9 or more). Compare this to the group who dropped out and the number of new friends they made in the church. In overview, the average active member could identify over 7 new friends in the church, the dropouts only 2.

After three months Mary could name five new friends she felt close to and went out with regularly. After six months she could identify nine new friends in the church, and she was beginning to feel quite comfortable in the groups and meetings in which she participated.

6. *An Assimilated Member Has a Task or Role Appropriate to His Spiritual Gift(s).* A "role" is an officially appointed or elected position for a person in the church, such as serving on an ad hoc committee, a board, welcoming visitors, leading a Bible study. A "task" is a special, goal-oriented assignment, such as helping with the planning of a special service, helping to repave the parking lot, working on a special missions project.

The more roles available to be filled, the more members can be involved. Once the roles have been created, church leaders are responsible to effectively assign roles to people with an appropriate spiritual gift. A wide variety of resources are available today to help members discover their spiritual gift(s).[2] As older members and new members begin to discover their spiritual gifts, they are invariably drawn to tasks for which God has equipped them.

Mary had accepted the role of incorporation coordinator in her Sunday School class. It was her duty to be the first to greet visitors who came to the class. She would learn

113

their names and introduce them to others in the class. Mary had also participated in a spiritual gifts discovery course and found she had the gift of hospitality. So she had become part of a "new neighbor" program in the community where church members invite those who are just moving into the community to their house for dinner. Mary is enjoying her new roles and feeling fulfilled as a contributing member of the church.

7. *An Assimilated Member Is Involved in a Fellowship Group.* One of the most meaningful, rewarding, growing experiences the new Christian will experience is in a smaller group of the church where the caring, loving fellowship of the Body can be experienced. This small-group involvement should be one of the first concerns of the church for its new members.

Organizing and regularly starting new groups for new members can be an effective strategy of assimilation. Often a new member will become active in a new group, as a "pioneer," where it might be difficult for him to break into an existing group where relationships are already established.

Mary fit easily into the Sunday School class where her two other friends were already members. She had even met several others in the class before, from previous church events she had attended. Mary also enrolled in the new members class and now six other new members and she were meeting for Bible study every Thursday morning.

8. *The Assimilated Member Feels Trusted by the Leadership of the Church.* Involvement is not enough. The ultimate test of assimilation is trust. Many members have dropped out, not because they weren't socially incorporated and practically involved but because psychologically they felt rebuffed. The lay leaders of the church did not trust them to chair a committee, be nominated for office, or give an opin-

ion on intensely internal matters of the fellowship. No amount of involvement can overcome the feeling of rejection when one believes he is not trusted. On the other hand, a sense of oneness with the church is experienced by the church member who feels he is genuinely trusted.

9. *The Assimilated Member Regularly Tithes to the Church.* "Where your treasure is, there your heart will be also" (Matt. 6:21). An important part of any member's responsibility to the church is financial. Regular stewardship should be stressed as a part of commitment to Christ and the church.

Mary is not wealthy, but she has faithfully tithed each month since she joined the church.

10. *The Assimilated Member Is Participating in the Great Commission.* A disciple of Jesus Christ is one who is actively involved in spreading the Good News to the members of his extended family. New Christians are some of the most enthusiastic people in the world. Many have just turned around 180° in their life-style and are so positively excited with their new faith that their enthusiasm often results in a natural pattern of friends and relatives coming to Christ and the church over a very short period of time. This natural desire to tell others should be encouraged.

One of the last topics in Mary's new member class was the importance of disciple-making as a part of Christ's call. Pastor Austin introduced the fact that each person has a group of close friends and relatives who are "potential disciples." Every person in the class was encouraged to identify the people in his extended family and develop disciple-making plans for reaching them. Mary had identified Cheryl Riley, a neighbor in the next door apartment, as a person to focus on. Mary had already begun building a stronger relationship with Cheryl and had told her of her new life in Christ.

Effective assimilation of new members should go hand in hand with an outreach strategy to friends and relatives. Through study, evaluation, planning, and regular monitoring of the assimilation process in your church, significant new levels of growth and ministry will be realized where new Christians can find a home and a place to grow.

10

The Master's Plan—
to the Ends of the Earth

It was already well into Saturday when Chuck finished
servicing his car. What had started out as a simple lube and
oil change at home, to save money, had turned into a horrendous task. Chuck was covered with grease from head to
toe, and bone weary. But at least he had done it all himself.

The hot shower felt good on his stiff, aching muscles

What had started out as a simple lube and oil change had turned into a
horrendous task.

and he was giving himself a generous covering of soap lather when Diane called.

"It's Pastor Austin. He has to talk to you immediately. He has to leave in five minutes for an emergency at County Hospital, but he insists he has to talk to you first."

"But, Diane, I'm all covered with soap."

Well, that's how Chuck ended up standing in a puddle of soapy water by the bedroom phone, clothed in a soggy, soapy robe. He tried to sound cheerful.

"Yes, Pastor, what can I do for you?"

Pastor Austin was calling to make sure Chuck could attend a special committee meeting the following morning. The only time he could arrange, which was "convenient" for everyone involved, was 30 minutes prior to the early service. "It won't take long, but we've got to get moving in some new areas."

"But, Pastor, I thought now that things were going so well with our disciple-making program we could start easing up a little bit. After all, at least half of my extended family is already discipled."

Pastor Austin gave what Chuck thought to be a surprising answer. "Well, Chuck, we're thankful for what's been done so far, but did you know that we have only just begun?"

"Pastor, what do you mean!"

"For one thing, all of us who have participated in the program need to get additional members into our extended families. And then we need to be sure disciple-making becomes the concern of all groups in the church. Then, I'm starting to wonder if we don't need to think about sponsoring at least one new church. Well, Chuck, I've got to get to the hospital. See you in the morning."

The surprising thing was that Chuck didn't act the least bit upset by this unexpected meeting. There are some who say Chuck Bradley isn't the same since he's been involved in

Diane says he's discovered that disciple-making is one of the most rewarding aspects of the Christian life.

The Master's Plan. Diane says he's discovered that disciple-making is one of the most rewarding aspects of the Christian life.

* * * * * * * * * *

As long as there are people yet unreached, Christ's command to make disciples remains . . .

Steps for Expanding Disciple-making

1. *Utilize New Christians.* As a church leader, how do you broaden your church's disciple-making endeavors? A natural place to begin is among the new converts. If you have met new Christians recently, you know that their enthusiasm and excitement with their new life in Christ is contagious. They are the happiest people in the world and want the world to

know. Life in Christ grants one a refreshingly new lease on life. So many old Christians have forgotten what it was like B.C. (before Christ).

The diagram below illustrates a surprising, yet natural, phenomenon that occurs in every church. The circle represents the church. The pyramid represents the world. A person at the bottom of the pyramid represents a person who is in the world but outside the church.

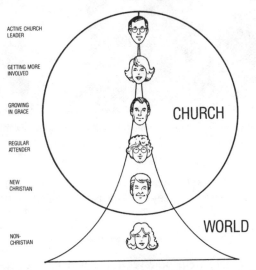

When the person becomes a Christian and church member, he still has a good number of contacts and friends in the world. As time passes, however, the now older Christian maintains fewer and fewer contacts in the world, and more and more contacts in the church. The reason is simply that as a Christian, he feels more comfortable associating with other Christians. New life in Christ is not often compatible with the life-style of old friends outside the church.

Many growing churches have discovered the fact that

new converts have more contacts with unchurched prospects than do longtime members. As a result, these churches have found ways to train the new Christians in how to effectively communicate the Good News to their friends.

2. *Expand to All Present Groups in the Church.* Effective disciple-making does not stop with new Christians trained and involved in reaching out. Disciple-making does not stop with only one segment of the congregation trained or involved. *The Master's Plan* calls for every disciple of Christ to communicate God's love and caring to his extended family.

This means helping each layperson identify the people in his extended family, to begin praying for them, caring for them, and planning to see these people come to Christ and the Church.

3. *Begin New Groups.* A third step in expanding the disciple-making process is to start new units. "New groups produce new growth."[1] Regularly starting new units (classes, groups, cells) significantly increases your church's effectiveness in disciple-making.

New groups should be designed with distinct appeal to certain "homogeneous" groups of people (newlyweds, young singles, senior singles, women reentering the job market, widows, etc.). As more diverse groups become part of the church, new people will be able to find a home in the larger Body.

4. *Start a New Church.* The "Great Commission Goal" is defined as: "A cell (church) of committed Christians in every community, in every city, and in every countryside throughout the world where people can hear and see the gospel demonstrated by their own intimates, in their own tongue, and thus have a reasonable opportunity to become disciples of Jesus Christ."[2]

The Great Commission cannot be fulfilled in this country with the number of churches that presently exist. In fact, the 336,000 churches in America today could double without

121

overchurching the country. Can this really be true when almost every community in America appears to be well churched, with innumerable church buildings and open doors almost anywhere? One tends to conclude that there are plenty of churches in America, plenty of empty pews, and plenty of room for everyone. Such a conclusion needs to be challenged. While it may seem that there are enough churches for everyone, enormous numbers of people are unchurched and will remain so if we expect existing churches to reach them. The reason is that there are many people in America who simply will not feel comfortable in existing churches. Different churches appeal to different kinds of people. And there are segments of people in nearly every part of the country to whom no existing church provides attractive alternatives for their lives. Or, to say it another way, your church will not appeal to every person in your community, nor will any other.

The solution to this problem is not to hope other churches in the area will respond to the unique needs of the "unreachable" people. The secret is to identify who those people are and start a church deliberately structured to reach them.

The illustration below presents some important insights into both the cost and the effectiveness of disciple-making endeavors with various "homogeneous" groups of people in your community. The closer the group is to the center of the circle, the less costly and effective disciple-making efforts will be by members of your church. The farther the groups are from the center circle, the more costly and less effective will be your disciple-making endeavors. By the time disciple-making efforts are focused on people in the far circles, the evangelism process has become one of the "missions." And every good missionary knows that the most effective strategy is to win receptive people, plant a new church among those people, and then assist them in reaching their own families and webs.

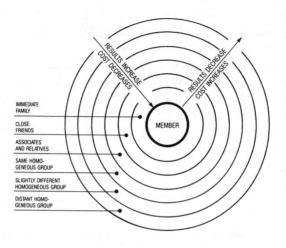

IMMEDIATE FAMILY

CLOSE FRIENDS

ASSOCIATES AND RELATIVES

SAME HOMO-GENEOUS GROUP

SLIGHTLY DIFFERENT HOMOGENEOUS GROUP

DISTANT HOMO-GENEOUS GROUP

MEMBER

RESULTS INCREASE COST DECREASES

RESULTS DECREASE COST INCREASES

Many churches like to think of themselves in the pattern of the New Testament church, doing things in a biblical fashion. But is a church really a New Testament church if it isn't planting churches? Being a real New Testament church means believing and doing what the New Testament church did. The New Testament church was tremendously concerned with, engaged in, and *successful* at establishing new congregations. Churches were planted in Jerusalem, Judea, and Samaria. Churches were planted in Galilee, Antioch, Rome, and in city after city around the Mediterranean. Toward the end of his life, Paul was heading toward Spain to begin planting churches there. Church multiplication was an essential part of New Testament life. Today, in a world where three out of four persons have yet to believe in Jesus Christ, if a congregation is not reproducing, it is not a New Testament church, no matter what it calls itself.[3]

Church planting begins with the conviction that it is God's will that His Church grow. Such a conviction grows into a deep concern for people in the community without Christ.

When these concerns permeate the people of God in the local congregation, beginning a new church becomes a real possibility.

Most churches discover that planting a daughter church is not actually the drain of resources on the mother church that perhaps they thought it would be. Rather it often proves to be a boost to growth, morale, and enthusiasm. Like the birth of a new baby, a brand-new congregation is a job to experience and be a part of.

If the vast mosaic of people in North America are going to be reached for Christ, existing churches not only need to grow themselves, but they also need to give priority to the multiplication of new churches.

5. *Reach Across Cultures.* The Great Commission, which Christ gave to His Church, was a command to disciple "to the ends of the earth." Most English versions translate the command of Christ in Matt. 28:19 to read: "make disciples of all *nations.*" But this is a mistranslation. The original Greek translation is to disciple *ta ethne. Ethne* does not mean the modern national states such as India, the United States, or China. *Ethne* means the ethnic units of mankind, all the mosaics and kinds of people in a nation, the variety of levels and subcultures of society. The Great Commission is a call to disciple every piece of the vast mosaic of humankind that makes up the 3 billion yet to believe.[4]

In referring to his own call, Paul wrote: "This gospel . . . is about Jesus Christ our Lord. Through him I received the privilege of a commission . . . to lead to faith and obedience men in all *ethne"* (Rom. 1:2, 4-5, NEB). The Great Commission will be fulfilled when every person has had a reasonable opportunity to see and hear the gospel from his own intimates, in his own culture, and is given a chance to repent, believe, and become part of a local Body of Christ.

Christians today have more responsibility than any previous generation to invest time, money, and people to reach out to "the ends of the earth" with the Good News.

Can the Great Commission be fulfilled?

We have come a long way since Christ left those few apostles with such a seemingly impossible task. There are now faithful Christians on every continent of the globe. There are Christian churches found in every country. It is not a question of *can* the Great Commission be fulfilled. It *is* being fulfilled. The question is whether you and your church will be a part. Will the Master return, as Christ illustrated in the parable of the talents, to find that your church has hidden its "treasure" and has nothing more to show? Or, will He return to find the treasure left in your care to be multiplied through faithful investment? And then He will say to you, "Well done, thou good and faithful servant."

* * * * * * * * * *

Mark Peters and his friend Bob Taylor walked down the steps of the high school. It was Friday evening. Mark and Bob had just finished playing in the church league basketball playoffs, helping their church to its first championship. They were exhilarated and exhausted as they headed toward their cars.

"Man, what a game!" reflected Mark.

"Yeah. What a season! Remember that first game?" laughed Bob.

"Don't remind me. Boy, did we get blown out of there."

"Well, we sure got our act together after that."

"You're coming to the celebration over at the church aren't you?" asked Mark.

"Well, I . . . I don't know," stammered Bob.

"Hey, come on," insisted Mark. "We couldn't have made it through the season without you."

"Well, OK. But I've got to get going soon."

125

"Great. I'll see you over there," said Mark as each got in his car and left the parking lot.

Mark had been a member of the church for nearly a year. He had originally been introduced to Christ by his brother-in-law, Jim Herman. Jim, as it turned out, had been reached through a fishing buddy named Pete. And, of course, Pete was Chuck Bradley's first extended family member to come to Christ and the church.

So Mark was the fourth generation tracing his "spiritual roots" back to Chuck Bradley's involvement, over three years earlier, in the Master's plan for making disciples. Even though they were in the same church, Chuck would probably never know the extent to which he had been indirectly responsible for Mark's own Christian commitment and involvement in the church. Or that Bob Taylor, now a member of Mark's own extended family, would soon respond to the caring of the church and the call of Christ.

Since those first days of the Master's plan, when Pastor Austin began meeting with various members and helping them share God's love with extended families, the church had seen considerable new vitality and growth. In fact, a new committee had been organized during the previous week to examine the possibility of planting a new church in the coming year. The existing facilities were getting cramped and the church had already started holding a second service.

What had happened to this church in the last three years? How and why did it move from an "average" church, doing basically "average church work," to a dedicated and growing church, equipping its lay members to fulfill the Great Commission in their world?

The secret was in laity mobilized for making disciples. Chuck's church had discovered that the key to reaching their world for Christ was in lay people convinced: (1) of the opportunity that existed all about them, and (2) that they could individually, and as a church, expect to see their friends, relatives, and associates become Christians and members of their church.

It was not just because they had read a book or participated in a special series of meetings. The reason Chuck's church began to realize its previously untapped possibilities was they had taken seriously important biblical insights as well as modern-day applications of how Christ's good news can be extended to the "uttermost parts of the earth." The laity had learned to communicate Christ's love and were using their natural networks for the expansion of His Church.

Of course, there was not a 100 percent success rate. Not all the members of the church who could have been were involved in making disciples. Some extended family members never found Christ or His love through the church. A few new members who came into the church dropped out through oversights in the church assimilation system. But as Chuck, Pete, and several others on the church board were discussing at the last meeting, the events that took place three years previously, which launched the new emphasis in equipping laity and making disciples, had marked a significant new direction for the church. Those events had contributed directly to a new level of morale among the members, and the beginning of exciting new heights of achievement for the congregation in fulfilling Christ's command to go . . . and make disciples.

Glossary

Assimilation—The process by which new Christians and church members come to understand and feel they are truly an accepted and trusted member of the fellowship.

Church-centered Disciple-making—An intentional strategy and priority of the church, which initiates disciple-making, trains members in disciple-making, plans regular opportunities for conversion, uses resources of the Body, creates support resources and incorporates new believers into the church.

Church Growth—An application of biblical, theological, social, and behavioral science principles to the local church and its surrounding community in an effort to influence and disciple the greatest number of people for Jesus Christ. Believing that "it is God's will that His Church grow and His lost children are found," Church Growth endeavors to formulate strategies, develop objectives, and apply proven principles of effective evangelism to the local church.

Decision—A personal commitment to receive Jesus Christ as Savior.

Disciple—A person who has made a commitment to Jesus Christ as Lord and Savior, who is learning and following His teachings, is identified in a meaningful relationship with His Body—the Church—and participating in its mission of spreading the gospel.

Effective Evangelism—Proclaiming Jesus Christ as God and Savior and persuading people to become His disciples and responsible members of His Church.

Extended Family—A church member's close friends, relatives, and associates who are not presently in Christ and the Church.

Incorporation—The process of involving new contacts with church people, programs, and facilities so they feel socially comfortable in the church environment.

Master's Plan for Making Disciples—A strategy of disciple-making that helps a church equip its members to identify and reach the people in their circles of influence for Christ and the Church.

Ministry Area—The area within a reasonable driving distance of a church.

New Testament Church—A church that intends to be like the churches described in the New Testament.

Oikos—The Greek word meaning "household." In the Graeco-Roman culture *oikos* described not only the immediate family in the house, but included friends, servants, servants' families, and even business associates.

Potential Congregation—The cumulative group of extended families of church members.

Receptivity, Periods of—Times when individuals, people, societies tend to be more open to the gospel message.

Spiritual Gifts—Special attributes given by the Holy Spirit to every member of the Body of Christ, according to God's grace.

Support Team—A group of church members who meet together regularly to encourage one another and learn how to more effectively communicate God's love to extended family members.

Webs—People of common kinship (the larger family), common friendship (friends, neighbors), and common associates (special interest, work relationships, recreation).

Witness (Noun)—One whose words and actions reflect the meaning that Christ and the Church give to his everyday experiences.

Witness (Verb)—The process by which a Christian communicates God's love.

Worshiping Congregation—Those people who are on the membership role of a church and/or who worship regularly with that body of believers.

Reference Notes

CHAPTER 1

1. Kenneth Van Wyk, "Educate for Church Growth," *Church Growth: America,* March/April 1978, 7.

2. Donald McGavran and Win Arn, *Back to Basics in Church Growth* (Wheaton, Ill.: Tyndale House, 1981), 108-09.

3. Robert E. Coleman, *The Mind of the Master* (Old Tappan, N.J.: Fleming H. Revell Co., 1977), 9.

4. McGavran and Arn, *Back to Basics,* 79.

5. Michael Green, *Evangelism in the Early Church* (Grand Rapids: Eerdmans, 1970), 210.

6. Ibid., 54.

CHAPTER 2

1. Ralph W. Neighbors, Jr., *Future Church* (Nashville: Broadman Press, 1980), 163.

2. Hans Walter Wolff, *Anthology of the Old Testament* (Philadelphia: Fortress Press, 1974), 215.

3. Kenneth Scott Latourette, *A History of the Expansion of Christianity, Volume I: The First Five Centuries* (New York: Harper, 1937), 116.

4. Donald A. McGavran, *The Bridges of God* (New York: Friendship Press, 1968), 27-28.

5. Charles Arn, Donald McGavran, Win Arn, *Growth: A New Vision for the Sunday School* (Pasadena, Calif.: Church Growth Press, 1980), 75-76.

6. Donald A. McGavran, *Understanding Church Growth* (Grand Rapids: Eerdmans, 1970), 359-63.

CHAPTER 3

1. W. Charles Arn, "The Friendship Factor," *Church Growth: America,* May/June 1981, 13.

CHAPTER 4

1. W. Charles Arn, "The Friendship Factor," *Church Growth: America,* May/June 1981, 13.

CHAPTER 5

1. Paul Tillich in *The Friendship Factor* (Minneapolis: Augsburg Publishing House, 1979), 109.

2. W. Charles Arn, "How to Find Receptive People," *The Pastor's Church Growth Handbook* (Pasadena, Calif.: Church Growth Press, 1979), 143.

CHAPTER 7

1. Alan Loy McGinnis, *The Friendship Factor* (Minneapolis: Augsburg Publishing House, 1979), 54.

2. Merlin R. Carothers, *Power in Praise* (Plainfield, N.J.: Logos International, 1972), 117.

3. Flavil R. Yeakley, Jr., *Why Churches Grow* (Arvada, Colo.: Christian Communications, 1979), 37.

CHAPTER 8

1. Win Arn, *The Pastor's Church Growth Handbook* (Pasadena, Calif.: Church Growth Press, 1979), 54.

2. *The Master's Plan Church Action Kit* has excellent and specific ideas to raise the disciple-making awareness of laity in a local congregation. Information on *The Master's Plan Church Action Kit* is available from the Institute for American Church Growth, 150 S. Los Robles, Suite 600, Pasadena, CA 91101.

3. Yeakley, *Why Churches Grow,* 66.

4. Interview with Rev. Robert Orr and Lyle Schaller, January, 1977, Pasadena, Calif.

CHAPTER 9

1. W. Charles Arn, "Friendship Factor," *Church Growth: America,* May/June 1981, 13.

2. An excellent self-study kit is available to work through the subject of spiritual gifts: *Spiritual Gifts for Building the Body.* Available from the Institute for American Church Growth, 150 S. Los Robles, Suite 600, Pasadena, CA 91101.

CHAPTER 10

1. Arn, McGavran, Arn, *Growth: A New Vision,* 105.

2. *Basic Growth Seminar Workbook* (Pasadena, Calif.: Institute for American Church Growth, 1979), 5.

3. Donald McGavran and Win Arn, *Ten Steps for Church Growth* (New York: Harper and Row, 1977), 96.

4. Ibid, 38.